DIY SCIENCE ENGINEERING

Over **20** incredible engineering projects to build at home

AUTUMN PUBLISHING

AUTUMN
PUBLISHING

Illustrated by Karl West
Written by Wednesday Jones

Designed by Simon Parker
Edited by Suzanne Fossey

Engineering Consultancy by Ed Walsh

Published in 2022
First published in the UK by Autumn Publishing
An imprint of Igloo Books Ltd
Cottage Farm, NN6 0BJ, UK
Owned by Bonnier Books
Sveavägen 56, Stockholm, Sweden

Manufactured in China. 0622 001
10 9 8 7 6 5 4 3 2 1

Library of Congress Cataloging-in-Publication
Data is available upon request.

ISBN 978-1-80108-761-2
autumnpublishing.co.uk
bonnierbooks.co.uk

CONTENTS

HOW TO BE AN ENGINEER

It's helpful to have a notebook or journal where you can write down your notes and thoughts about your experiments and the world around you.

OBSERVE

Carry your engineering notebook around with you and take notes on things that you see. If you go for a walk, write down or draw different types of buildings or vehicles you spot. The more you notice about the world around you, the more you'll be able to think of new questions.

ASK QUESTIONS

How do really tall buildings stay standing? How do elevators and escalators work? Keep thinking of questions and writing them down. If you find out the answer later, you can always add that to your notebook, too!

TRY TO GUESS WHAT WILL HAPPEN (BEFORE IT HAPPENS)

This is called making a prediction. What will happen if you try to build a car out of plastic? What will happen if you change the shape of the rocket or use a different chemical to make a bouncy ball? Write down what you think will happen before you do the experiment.

DO THE EXPERIMENT

Make notes on how you do the experiment. All sorts of things can make a difference on how the results turn out. Did you use glue instead of tape, or swap the order of the steps? Write down what happened. If you took any measurements, write them down. Draw pictures or take photos to tape into your notebook.

WHAT IF IT DOESN'T WORK LIKE IT SHOULD?

An important aspect of being an engineer is problem solving. Sometimes the experiment won't work perfectly right away, so you will need to put your engineer's hat on and look at how you can make it better. This is something engineers need to be good at. Your engineering notebook will be very helpful.

COME UP WITH NEW QUESTIONS

Use your results to think up other questions. How would you do things differently next time? What do you think would change? Start the process all over again!

This process is known as the scientific method. People have been following these steps for over a thousand years, and it has helped scientists figure out the answers to questions from "What happens if I hit this thing with a big rock?" to "What shape is the Universe?"

NOTES FOR GROWN-UPS

Engineering is a big topic, so don't worry if you don't know all the answers! If your child asks you something you're not sure about, think together about how you can change the experiment to find out, or where you can look it up.

When doing these experiments with your child, keep things light and fun and let your child take the lead. Help them with the tricky parts, ask lots of questions, and make sure they stay safe.

 **WARNING**

Some of the experiments in this book involve potential hazards such as heat or sharp implements. The publisher strongly recommends that parents / guardians supervise their children during ALL activities, paying special attention to stages marked with a triangle warning sign.

Whenever starting on one of these experiments, always read through the instructions and consider what safety precautions are necessary. It is a good idea to involve your child with this discussion: identifying risks and taking sensible precautions is a key part of laboratory life. Talk about questions like whether it would be best to wear protective clothing such as goggles or rubber gloves, and whether it is best to do the experiment inside or outside in a safe place. Always use your judgment and stay safe.

EXHILARATING EXPERIMENTS

EXHILARATING EXPERIMENTS

Have you ever wondered how a roller coaster car goes so fast, or how a parachute really works? Have you looked at something and thought "it's good, but I can make it better?" If so, then you are thinking like an engineer.

What's the first question every engineer should ask? No, it's not "where are the snacks?" It's "What is the problem that needs solving?"

Use these experiments to help you look at problems (like how to reach things up high, or how to make a call using just string and paper cups) and find new and exciting ways to solve them.

MONSTER JAWS

Do your parents keep the good snacks way up high, out of your reach? Well, not anymore with this monstrously fun grabber.

YOU WILL NEED
- 13 craft sticks
- white glue
- 13 paper fasteners
- scissors
- thick cardboard
- an adult with a drill to do the hard work
- 2 rubber bands
- pencil

STEP 1

Grab ten craft sticks and ask an adult to make three holes in each one using a drill. The holes need to be big enough to fit a paper fastener through.

STEP 2

Line up two of the craft sticks and push the paper fastener through the center holes. Open up the fastener to secure it. Repeat using the other craft sticks so that you have five Xs.

STEP 4

When you've connected all the Xs, open and close your grabber a few times to make sure the movement is smooth.

STEP 3

Take two Xs and line up the top of one with the bottom of another (it doesn't matter which way they go). Push a paper fastener through the holes in each side so that the X's are all connected to each other.

SNAP!

SNAP!

SNAP!

STEP 5

Cut another craft stick in half. Glue both halves of the craft stick to the top of your grabber.

STEP 6

Using the thick cardboard, draw and cut out some scary teeth. Glue them onto the craft sticks you added in step 5. Why not add googly eyes and some scary scales?

STEP 7

Glue one craft stick on either side of the bottom of the grabber to make handles. You can wrap these in rubber bands or grip tape if you choose, to make your grip better. Now, go find hidden things!

HOW DOES IT WORK?

Levers are engineering tools for turning small movements into big ones (or vice versa). A lever is a solid stick or pole that turns around a pivot. Your grabber is made of lots of levers (craft sticks) turning on lots of pivots (paper fasteners). The levers push on each other, turning the small movement your hands make pushing the handles into a big movement for your grabber's snapping jaws.

WHEELIE FUN!

Astound your friends with your magnificent strength by carrying heavy objects around without breaking a sweat. It'll be wheelie fun.

YOU WILL NEED

- 1 shoebox
- 2 sticks of wood 1 inch wide and at least 20 inches long
- 1 empty thread spool
- 1 piece of cardboard
- something heavy
- pencil
- clear tape
- scissors

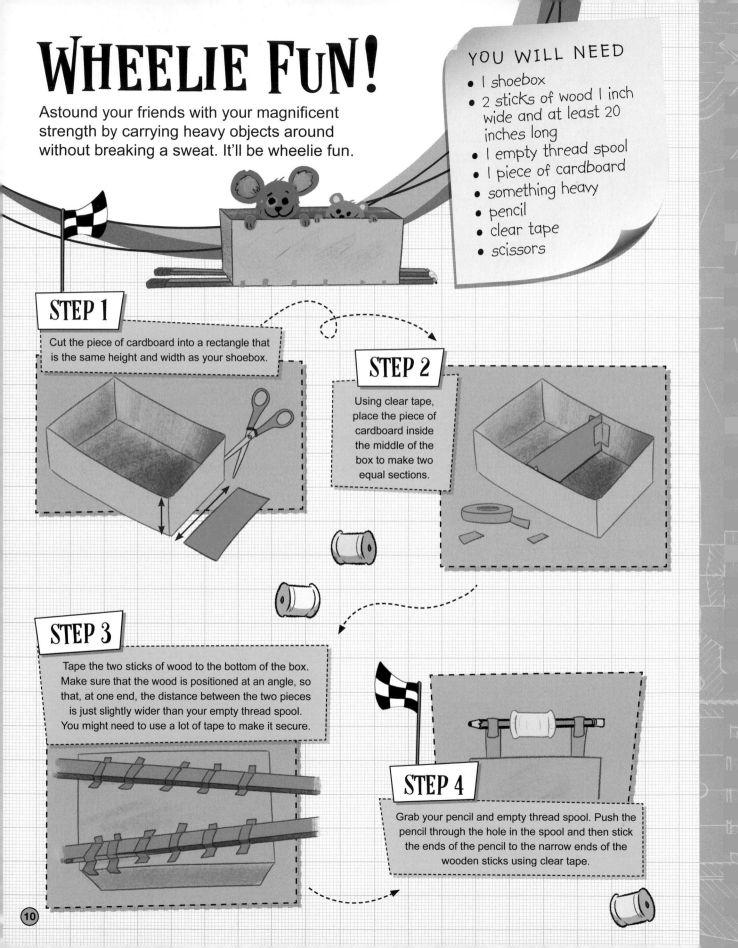

STEP 1

Cut the piece of cardboard into a rectangle that is the same height and width as your shoebox.

STEP 2

Using clear tape, place the piece of cardboard inside the middle of the box to make two equal sections.

STEP 3

Tape the two sticks of wood to the bottom of the box. Make sure that the wood is positioned at an angle, so that, at one end, the distance between the two pieces is just slightly wider than your empty thread spool. You might need to use a lot of tape to make it secure.

STEP 4

Grab your pencil and empty thread spool. Push the pencil through the hole in the spool and then stick the ends of the pencil to the narrow ends of the wooden sticks using clear tape.

STEP 5

Put your heavy, completely unbreakable item in the top section of the shoebox nearest to your hands. Then, lift the box using the handles. Is it easy to lift?

Move the heavy thing to the front section. Is it much easier to lift now?

HOW DOES IT WORK?

Did you notice it's easier to lift the object when it is in the part of the box that's farther from your hands? That's because the handles of the wheelbarrow are actually long levers. Levers turn a big, easy movement at the top end (your hands lifting the handles) into a smaller but more powerful movement at the bottom end. The thread spool is the turning point (pivot), and helps you move the load along.

When you pick up the handles of the wheelbarrow and raise it, you are actually applying effort to the lever. When you apply force (by giving it a little push) the wheel will start rolling, allowing you to move your heavy load with ease.

START

FINISH

PAPER CUP TELEPHONES

Do you wish you had your very own phone? Well, all you have to do is follow these steps. Briiing, briiing . . .

STEP 1

Ask an adult to use the pushpin to make a small hole in the bottom of each cup.

STEP 2

Make sure that the bottoms of the cups are facing each other. Poke the ends of the string through the holes.

STEP 3

Tie a paper clip to each end of the string.

HOW DOES IT WORK?

We hear sounds when our ears pick up vibrations in the air, called sound waves. The cool thing is, those vibrations can travel through other things as well as air! When you speak into your cup, the sound waves are transferred down the string into the cup at the opposite end. If you had three or four cups and joined the string from each one together, you could have a conversation with more than one person. Each person's string has to be tight, though!

STEP 4

Pull the string tight so that the paper clips are pulled to the bottom of the cups. Take turns speaking into one of the cups. Hold the other cup to your ear to listen.

WHAT NEXT?

Why not try using different materials? Can you still hear the other "caller" if you use a plastic water bottle? What about if you use wool or yarn instead of string?

PADDLE AWAY

The challenge, if you choose to accept it, is to design and build a paddleboat out of everyday items. The paddleboat needs to be able to travel in a straight line as far as possible.

STEP 1

Wrap a rubber band around the middle of your container, and push the pencils through, one on each side. Wrap one rubber band around each end of the pencils. You may need to ask someone to hold the pencils in place while you do this.

STEP 2

Cut two rectangles out the sides of the empty milk bottle. They should be the same width as your plastic container.

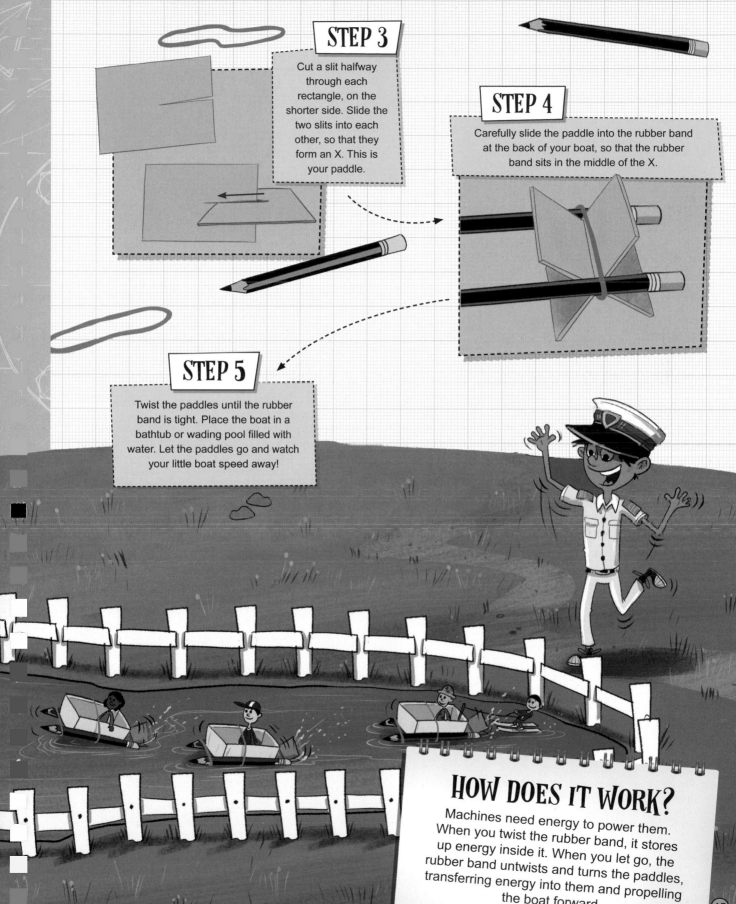

STEP 3

Cut a slit halfway through each rectangle, on the shorter side. Slide the two slits into each other, so that they form an X. This is your paddle.

STEP 4

Carefully slide the paddle into the rubber band at the back of your boat, so that the rubber band sits in the middle of the X.

STEP 5

Twist the paddles until the rubber band is tight. Place the boat in a bathtub or wading pool filled with water. Let the paddles go and watch your little boat speed away!

HOW DOES IT WORK?

Machines need energy to power them. When you twist the rubber band, it stores up energy inside it. When you let go, the rubber band untwists and turns the paddles, transferring energy into them and propelling the boat forward.

BLAST OFF!

Making this rocket will be an absolute BLAST! Just make sure you are clear of breakable items, windows, and people. Okay, ready for launch. In 3 ... 2 ... 1 ...

YOU WILL NEED

- 2 cardboard tubes
- 3 sheets of cardstock
- 1 straw (or a wooden chopstick or pencil)
- 1 rubber band
- white glue
- scissors
- clear tape

STEP 1

Cut one of the cardboard tubes all along one side. Roll it so that the tube becomes smaller (about half size), then use some tape it to hold in place.

STEP 2

On your sheet of card, draw around one end of the tube from step 1. Cut the circle out and stick it to the end of the tube using clear tape.

STEP 3

Using your white glue, stick the straw onto the cardstock circle.

STEP 4

Take the other cardboard tube and cut two slits in one end, about $1/3$ inch long and $3/4$ inch apart. Cut two more slits on the same end, directly across from the first two.

STEP 5

Put the smaller tube inside the larger one. Loop the center of the rubber band through the slits in the larger tube, then pull the ends down and over the ends of the straw. Put some tape over the slits to reinforce the cardboard tabs.

STEP 6

Roll a piece of cardstock into a tube and stick it in place with tape. This tube should just fit inside the larger cardboard tube.

STEP 7

Draw a large circle on another piece of card. Cut it out using your scissors and then cut a slit into the center of the circle.

STEP 8

Pull the edges of the slit together to make a cone, and secure with clear tape. Glue the cone to the top of the cardstock tube you rolled in step 6.

STEP 9

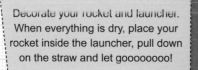

Decorate your rocket and launcher. When everything is dry, place your rocket inside the launcher, pull down on the straw and let goooooooo!

HOW DOES IT WORK?

When you pull down on the straw, you are stretching the rubber band and storing energy in it. When you let go, the energy is transferred to the rocket, making it fly upward. Wheeeeeee!

SUPER BOING!

Say goodbye to boring bouncy balls because it's time to make your own superbouncy, superfun, engineering-powered ball. Super!

YOU WILL NEED
- Contact lens solution (containing boric acid)
- PVA glue
- baking soda
- food coloring
- plastic cup
- tablespoon
- teaspoon
- an adult

STEP 1

Spoon three tablespoons of PVA glue into the plastic cup.

STEP 2

Next, add five to ten drops of food coloring to the glue.

STEP 3

Carefully spoon in one teaspoon of baking soda and stir well.

STEP 4

Add two teaspoons of the contact lens solution. Once again, you'll need to stir this in really well.

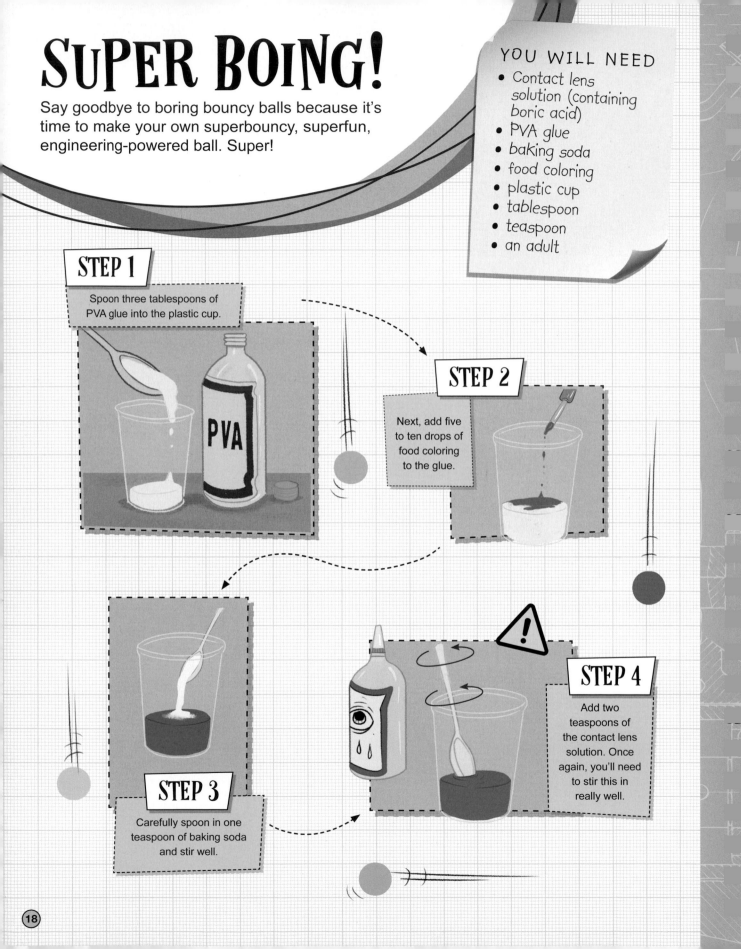

Empty the mixture out of the cup and onto a covered surface.

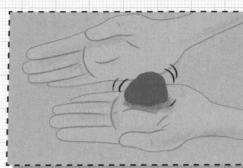

STEP 6

Time to get hands on! Roll the mixture between your hands so that it forms a ball. If it's a little too sticky, pour some more contact lens solution over the mixture.

STEP 7

Take your ball outside. Throw it high into the air and look incredibly smug as it bounces around.

HOW DOES IT WORK?

Everything around you is made up of tiny particles called molecules. Some things, like water, have quite small molecules, while others have molecules shaped like long thin chains. These chain-shaped molecules are called polymers, and when they tangle up and stick together, they can make things that are tough and springy, like your bouncy ball.

Polymers are important chemicals and are all around us. Natural polymers include things like wool and silk, and synthetic (human-made) polymers are found in plastics, glues, bulletproof vests, and even the coating on frying pans!

EGGS AWAY!

Build a parachute to protect an egg when you chuck it out the window. Sergeant Eggsy at your service!

YOU WILL NEED

- 1 sheet of cardstock
- 1 hard-boiled egg
- clear tape
- scissors
- hole punch
- 2 clear sandwich bags
- bubble wrap
- string
- ruler

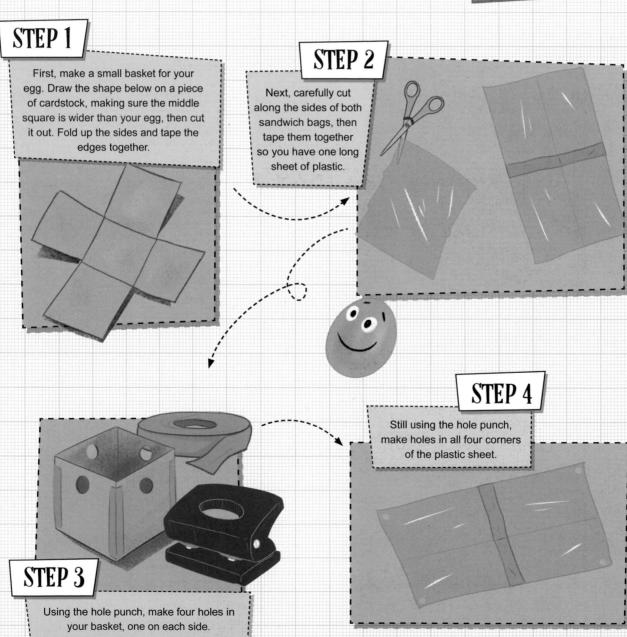

STEP 1

First, make a small basket for your egg. Draw the shape below on a piece of cardstock, making sure the middle square is wider than your egg, then cut it out. Fold up the sides and tape the edges together.

STEP 2

Next, carefully cut along the sides of both sandwich bags, then tape them together so you have one long sheet of plastic.

STEP 4

Still using the hole punch, make holes in all four corners of the plastic sheet.

STEP 3

Using the hole punch, make four holes in your basket, one on each side.

STEP 5

Cut four 12-inch pieces of string. Tie one piece of string to each corner of the plastic sheet. Tie the other ends to the sides of the parachute basket.

STEP 6

Before you start throwing eggs out of windows, it's a good idea to test the parachute. Put a small pebble in the basket to mimic the weight of the egg. Check that the parachute opens correctly and falls slowly.

STEP 7

When everything is working correctly, give the hard-boiled egg a little life jacket by wrapping it in bubble wrap and put it in the basket. If your basket is too big, put bubble wrap in the gaps.

STEP 8

Now drop your parachute from a series of different heights. Check that your parachutist has made it down intact between each drop and isn't too scrambled. Get it? Scrambled. Ha.

WHAT NEXT?

This experiment is a little different than the others. As you work through the steps, try to think of ways you could improve the design. Can you think of a way to make the parachute stay in the air longer?

If you could change your design, what would you do? If you could have any material you wanted, what would you use?

Use your engineer's notebook to record the different ways you could improve this experiment. Keep a record of what works and what doesn't.

HOW DOES IT WORK?

There are two forces acting on your little egg parachutist: the force of gravity pulling it down, and air resistance, which is the slowing-down force created by the air it has to push aside as it falls. The bigger the area of a falling object, the bigger the air resistance, and the slower it falls. Parachutes add lots of area, adding air resistance so your egg doesn't fall too fast.

MOVIE MAKER

What does every kid dream of? Their own movie theater and unlimited snacks, right? This will help with the movie theater part. As for the snacks, well, that's up to you.

ONE

YOU WILL NEED
- 1 small cardboard box
- 1 sheet of cardboard
- 1 magnifying glass
- scissors
- clear tape
- 1 smartphone (you can use a tablet, but you will need a bigger box)
- a blank wall
- pencil
- black paint
- paint brush
- an adult

STEP 1

Place the magnifying glass on one side of the cardboard box and use a pencil to draw around it.

STEP 2

Ask an adult to help you cut a hole in the box that is slightly smaller than the circular pencil lines.

ONE

STEP 3

Use a piece of cardboard to cut and fold a stand for the phone. Secure it with a piece of clear tape.

STEP 4

Paint the inside of the box with the black paint—all of it needs to be painted, including the inside of the flaps.

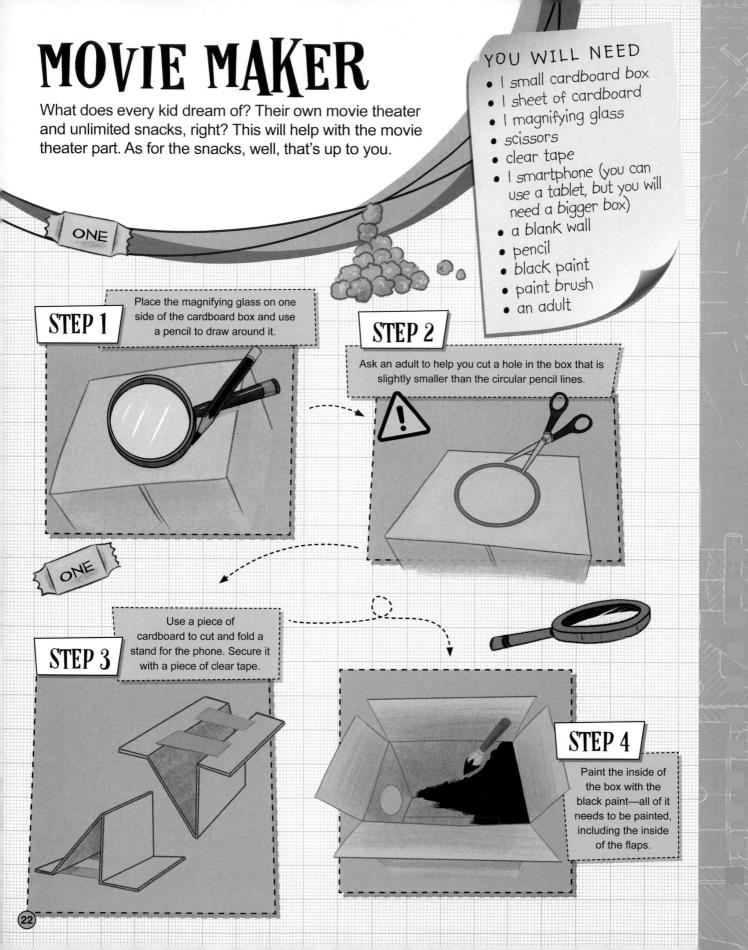

STEP 5

Tape the magnifying glass inside the box so that the lens is aligned with the hole in the box.

STEP 6

Slide the phone stand into the box. Turn on the film and lock the smartphone screen so it cannot turn. Put the phone upside down on the stand and turn the magnifying end toward a wall.

HOW DOES IT WORK?

The human eye has a lens in it that takes in light and guides it to the vision center in our brain. The magnifying lens in this experiment works like the lens in your eye—it catches the light rays that the smartphone screen gives out and then bends them toward the wall.

Remember when you turned the smartphone upside down? This is because, when a lens catches the light rays, it crosses them over and turns them around. Our eyes do this, too, and everything we see is sent to our brain upside down. It's our brain's job to turn it all the right way around so that we don't see the world upside down.

This experiment will involve some trial and error. To get a clear image on the wall, you might need to try moving the projector closer to or farther away from the wall. The room will also have to be very dim and the smartphone's screen will have to be at maximum brightness.

THE SNACK EXPRESS

Who doesn't want their favorite snacks delivered whenever they want?

STEP 1

Cut the flaps off your extra large cardboard box. Turn the box on its end and draw a large rectangle in the center. Ask an adult to help you cut it out and put the piece of cardboard to one side.

STEP 2

Cut two craft sticks in half and ask an adult to help you make holes in all four rounded ends using a drill.

STEP 3

Slide an empty thread spool onto a wooden skewer and place it in the center using white glue or modeling clay.

STEP 4

Push two of the craft stick halves from step 2 onto one end of the wooden skewer. Pull them apart so that they form an upside-down V-shape, and tape or glue them to the side of the box. There should be a $^3/_4$ inch gap between the wooden skewer and the top of the box. Repeat with the other side. The thread spool should hover over the rectangular hole in the box.

STEP 5

Cut a circle out of the corrugated cardboard. Ask an adult to help you cut the second wooden skewer into six 1-inch pieces. Push these into the side of the cardboard circle, so that it looks like a ship's wheel, and glue them in place.

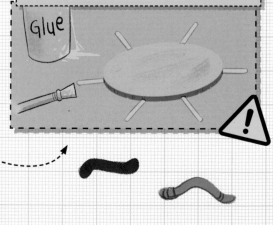

Glue

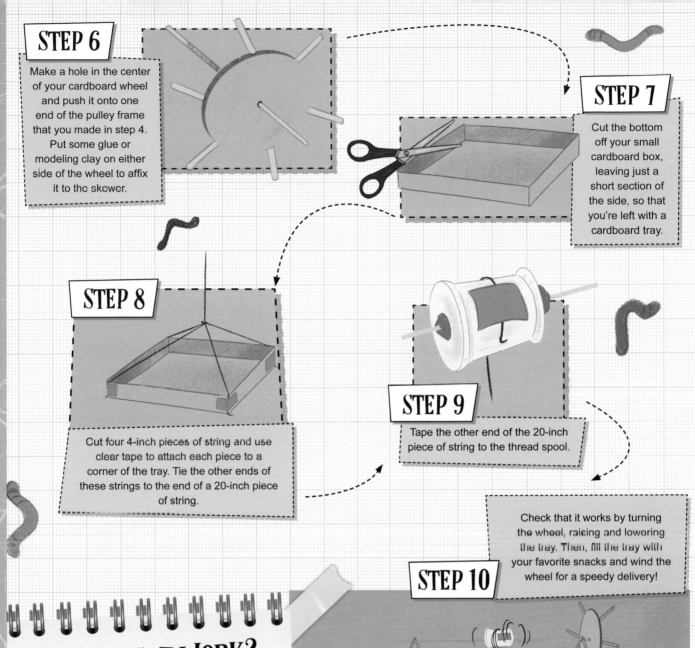

STEP 6

Make a hole in the center of your cardboard wheel and push it onto one end of the pulley frame that you made in step 4. Put some glue or modeling clay on either side of the wheel to affix it to the skewer.

STEP 7

Cut the bottom off your small cardboard box, leaving just a short section of the side, so that you're left with a cardboard tray.

STEP 8

Cut four 4-inch pieces of string and use clear tape to attach each piece to a corner of the tray. Tie the other ends of these strings to the end of a 20-inch piece of string.

STEP 9

Tape the other end of the 20-inch piece of string to the thread spool.

STEP 10

Check that it works by turning the wheel, raising and lowering the tray. Then, fill the tray with your favorite snacks and wind the wheel for a speedy delivery!

HOW DOES IT WORK?

This kind of machine is called a winch. Winches are used in various ways, often with an electric motor doing the hard work of turning the wheel. Winches are used to pull broken-down cars onto the back of rescue trucks or to pull boats out of the water.

Be careful, though—by winding the tray up you are storing energy in it. If you don't believe this, just let go of the wheel and watch the tray descend, along with any snacks that are still on board!

CHALLENGES AND GAMES

CHALLENGES AND GAMES

Engineering isn't all tall buildings, futuristic cars, and funky furniture. It's also part of the playground in the local park, the most popular slide at school, and the games that you play.

From a pinball machine to a basketball court, a football goal to a paper airplane, every section of a game is carefully designed and tested by an engineer to make sure it all moves as planned. Without the vital planning stage, none of these games would work.

ROLL UP, ROLL UP

Read all about a new fashion trend: newspaper furniture!
No, seriously, this is all about sitting on some old
newspaper. Sounds simple, right? WRONG!

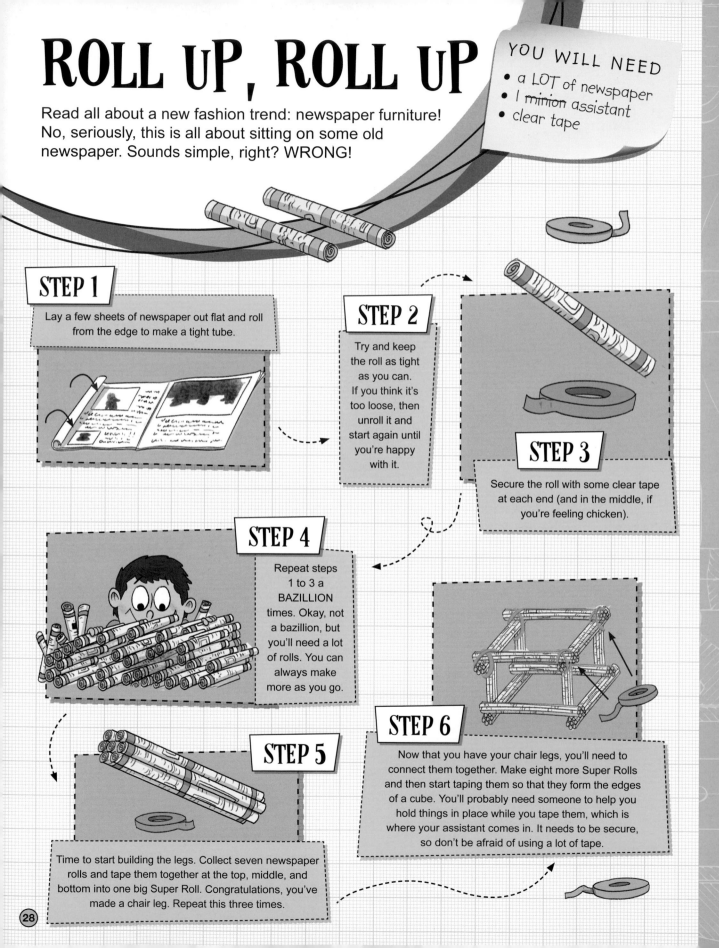

STEP 1

Lay a few sheets of newspaper out flat and roll
from the edge to make a tight tube.

STEP 2

Try and keep
the roll as tight
as you can.
If you think it's
too loose, then
unroll it and
start again until
you're happy
with it.

STEP 3

Secure the roll with some clear tape
at each end (and in the middle, if
you're feeling chicken).

STEP 4

Repeat steps
1 to 3 a
BAZILLION
times. Okay, not
a bazillion, but
you'll need a lot
of rolls. You can
always make
more as you go.

STEP 5

Time to start building the legs. Collect seven newspaper
rolls and tape them together at the top, middle, and
bottom into one big Super Roll. Congratulations, you've
made a chair leg. Repeat this three times.

STEP 6

Now that you have your chair legs, you'll need to
connect them together. Make eight more Super Rolls
and then start taping them so that they form the edges
of a cube. You'll probably need someone to help you
hold things in place while you tape them, which is
where your assistant comes in. It needs to be secure,
so don't be afraid of using a lot of tape.

STEP 7

The stool might be strong, but if you sit on it now it will twist and collapse. To stop this you need to add some strength. Using Super Rolls, make some triangle supports and tape them across the sides of your cube.

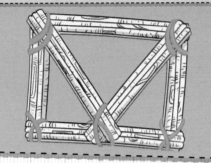

STEP 8

It's up to you to decide if your chair needs a back. If it does, remember it won't be holding much weight, so it doesn't have to be as strong as the base of the chair.

STEP 9

Once you've turned a pile of newspapers into modern art, carefully sit down on the chair. If you're not quite sure it's going to hold, you could put some pillows, a blanket, or your little brother under it to break your fall (Joking! Little brothers aren't squishy enough.)

WHAT NEXT?

Did it work or did the chair collapse when you sat on it? If it collapsed, try again, and experiment with different shapes like hexagons, or with more Super Rolls and supports. Engineering is all about trial and error, so this could be a good experience for your future career as a theme park-builder extraordinaire!

HOW DOES IT WORK?

Engineers call the weight an object can hold the load. In this experiment, you are the load!

Some shapes are better at bearing a load than others. Rectangles and squares are easily bent out of shape by a heavy load, but triangles are much harder to break. By connecting the joints of your chair with triangle supports—trusses—you added strength to the square shapes.

But how can flimsy paper support the weight of a person? The answer lies in the tubes. By layering up lots of flimsy things together, you can make one strong thing. Tubes of paper are very hard to squish by pushing on the ends. Just don't try and sit on one lengthways!

TARGET TRAINING

Size isn't everything and this tiny dart packs quite a punch. So put on your best superhero gear and ambush your enemies*.

* For the sake of this experiment, the tin cans are your enemies. Never aim your bow at people, animals, or breakable things.

YOU WILL NEED
- clear tape
- white glue
- straws
- 1 rubber band
- 18 craft sticks
- scissors
- markers
- 6 empty tin cans
- plain paper
- pom-poms

STEP 1

Ask an adult to cut the rounded ends off a craft stick. Then measure and cut the craft stick into seven equal pieces. It doesn't matter what size the pieces are, just that they're all the same size.

STEP 2

Glue the seven pieces of craft stick on top of each other to create a stack. Repeat with four more craft sticks.

Glue

STEP 3

When your stacks have completely dried, it's time to build your bow. Glue the limbs together so that they look like the picture. Start with the center piece and move outward.

STEP 4

Glue three more sticks on each side, as in the picture below. These will help to reinforce your bow.

STEP 5

Cut the last craft stick in half and glue the pieces onto the ends of the bow, so that they stick outward.

STEP 6

Once the ends are completely dry, loop a rubber band around them.

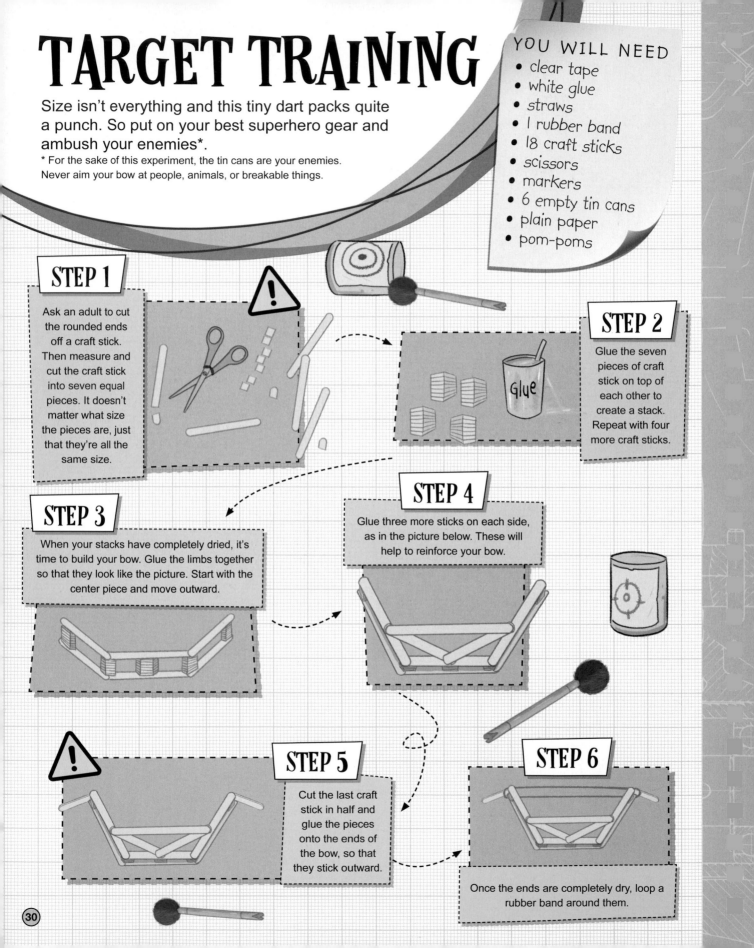

STEP 7

Wrap one end of each of your straws with sticky tape, and glue a pom-pom to the other end. Carefully cut V-shaped notches in the opposite ends.

Use your markers to draw targets on six strips of paper and tape them around the six empty tin cans. These are your "enemies".

STEP 8

STEP 9

To fire your arrow, put the notch in the arrow in the middle of the rubber band. Hold onto the arrow and pull back on the rubber band until you can't pull it back any more. Aim toward your stack of targets, pull back, and let go!

HOW DOES IT WORK?

It's a fact, triangles are the strongest shape. If you press down hard enough on a square, it will collapse, but the only way for a triangle to change its shape is if it breaks. The triangles you made out of craft sticks are called trusses. They act as reinforcements, allowing your bow to keep its shape, even when you pull back really hard on the rubber band. Look out for triangular trusses in other examples of engineering, like bridges and cranes.

BULLSEYE!

PINBALL WIZARD

Kick it old-school with this superfun arcade game. The aim is to score as many points as you can, so that you become the ultimate pinball champion.

15

STEP 1

On a large piece of cardboard, use your ruler and a pencil to draw the pieces you'll need for your pinball machine. When you have drawn all the pieces you need, use some scissors to cut them out.

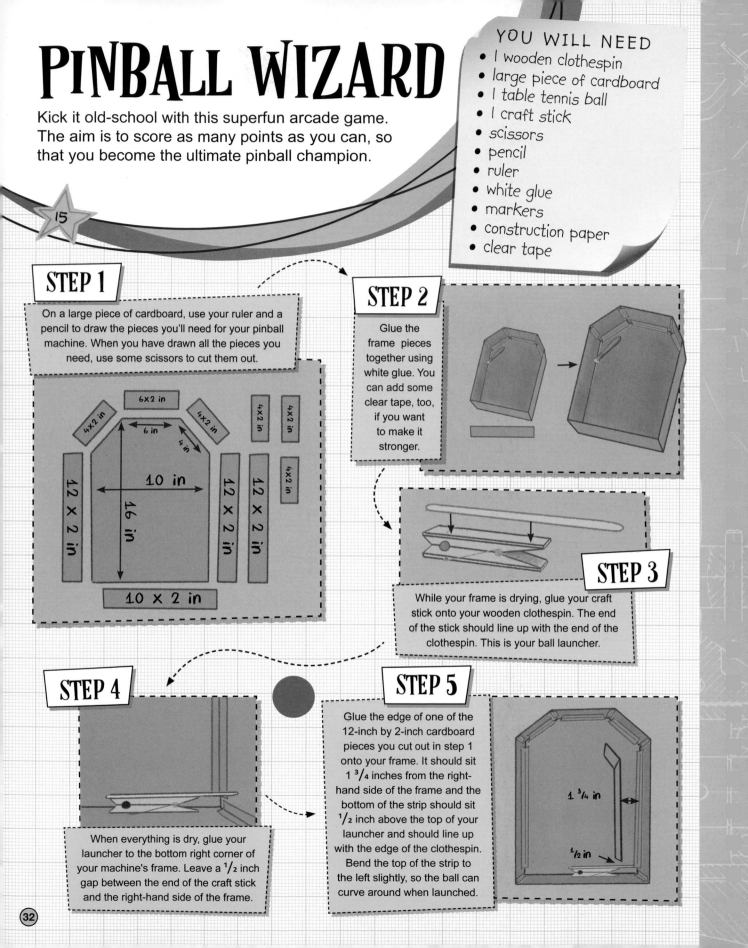

6x2 in

4x2 in

4x2 in

4x2 in

4x2 in

6 in

4 in

4x2 in

10 in

16 in

12 x 2 in

12 x 2 in

12 x 2 in

10 x 2 in

STEP 2

Glue the frame pieces together using white glue. You can add some clear tape, too, if you want to make it stronger.

STEP 3

While your frame is drying, glue your craft stick onto your wooden clothespin. The end of the stick should line up with the end of the clothespin. This is your ball launcher.

STEP 4

When everything is dry, glue your launcher to the bottom right corner of your machine's frame. Leave a $^1/_2$ inch gap between the end of the craft stick and the right-hand side of the frame.

STEP 5

Glue the edge of one of the 12-inch by 2-inch cardboard pieces you cut out in step 1 onto your frame. It should sit 1 $^3/_4$ inches from the right-hand side of the frame and the bottom of the strip should sit $^1/_2$ inch above the top of your launcher and should line up with the edge of the clothespin. Bend the top of the strip to the left slightly, so the ball can curve around when launched.

1 $^3/_4$ in

$^1/_2$ in

STEP 6

Take three of the 4-inch by 2-inch pieces and bend them into semicircles. Glue the edges of each onto the frame to make the scoring areas.

STEP 7

On construction paper, use some markers to draw your scoring system and add some other decorations. The bottom scoring area is the hardest to reach, so should be the most points.

STEP 8

Cut another piece of cardboard that's 30 inches by 10 inches wide.

STEP 9

Fold the strip of cardboard into a wedge shape and tape the ends together.

STEP 11

To play, drop your ball in the channel to the right so that it rests on the launcher. Press down on the very end of the craft stick and let go. The ball will fire upward and rocket into the scoring area, hopefully earning you big points.

STEP 10

Glue the back of your machine to the top of the wedge. The bottom of the machine should line up with the bottom edge of the wedge.

HOW DOES IT WORK?

When you press down on the craft stick to launch the ball, you are storing energy in the spring. Releasing the end of the craft stick transfers all this energy to the ball. It should travel to the top of the machine and then roll back. With skill you should be able to give it just enough energy to follow a path down to the high scoring areas.

SOCCER FUN

Challenge your friends, enemies, even the mailman to a game of soccer. Spin the rods and kick some ball!

YOU WILL NEED
- 1 cardboard box
- 12 clothespins
- 4 long wooden dowels (4 inches wider than the box)
- 1 table tennis ball
- 4 rubber bands
- paint
- a paintbrush
- scissors
- an adult
- ruler
- pencil

STEP 1

First, paint the back and front of your clothespins to look like soccer players—six per team. The hole-end of the clothespin is the head. Bonus points for funny expressions.

STEP 2

Cut the flaps off your cardboard box. Ask an adult to help you cut a rectangle from each end of the box—these are the goals.

STEP 3

Measure the side of the box. Make four holes in each side with the pointy end of a pencil, equal distance apart and about 2 ³/₄ inches from the bottom of the box.

2 ³/₄ in

STEP 4

Decorate the inside of your box to look like a soccer field. Don't forget to mark the center circle and the goal lines.

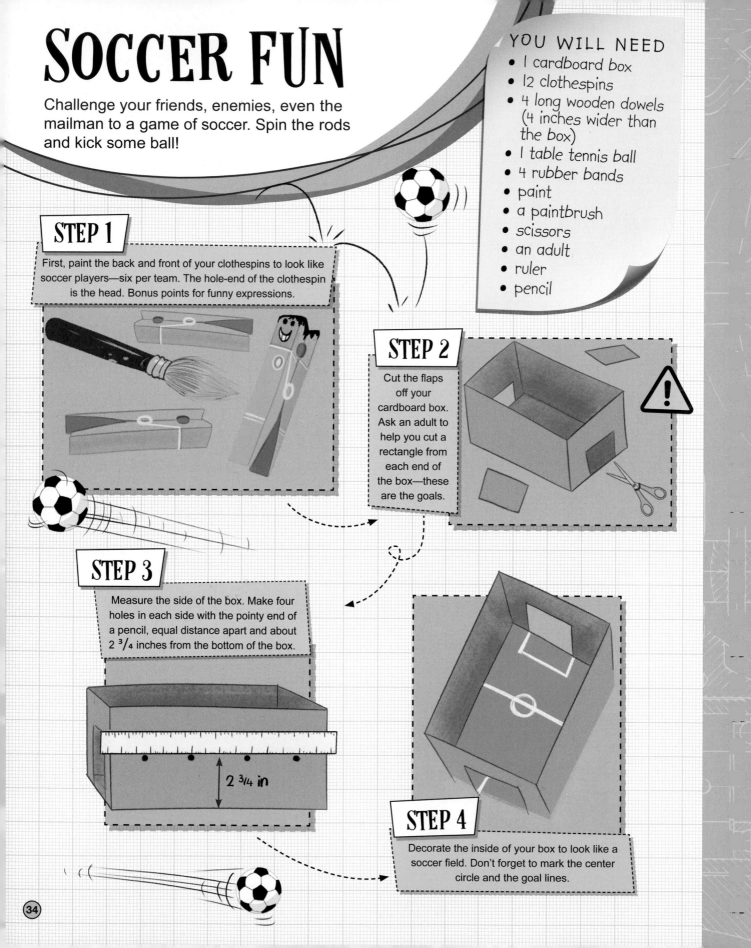

HOW DOES IT WORK?

This game is all about friction and forces. The clothespin players grip on the rods by friction. When the players hit the ball, the force they give it has to be big enough to send it down the table, but it has to be in the right direction, too. You have to not only twist the rod to make the players hit the ball, but also slide the rod in and out so you can hit the ball in the right place. Move quickly, though, as your opponent is ready to apply a force in the opposite direction.

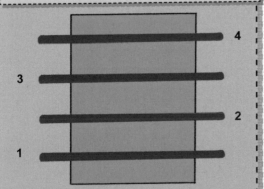

STEP 7

Drop the table tennis ball in the center. Wait for the whistle and then get spinning!

STEP 5

Push your four wooden dowels through the holes and wiggle them around so that they spin easily. Wrap a rubber band around the left-hand end of rods 1 and 3, and around the right-hand end of rods 2 and 4.

3

4

1

2

STEP 6

Clip three clothespin players from one team to rods 1 and 3, and three from the other team to rods 2 and 4. The clothes peg players should grip the rods tightly and not spin around. If they do spin, take the players off and glue little strips of cardboard (or felt, if you have some) around the rods where you want the players to sit. Once dry, put the players back into their positions.

4

3

2

1

(35)

GUMDROP TOWERS

Using only toothpicks and gumdrops, can you and your friends each build a gumdrop tower that will hold the weight of a book? Winner gets to eat all the gumdrops!

STEP 1

First, decide what shape your tower is going to be. One of you could try a square base, and another could use a triangular design. If there are more of you, add in more shapes: hexagons, pentagons, or even dodecahedrons for those feeling adventurous (and a little show-off-y, let's be honest.)

STEP 2

Now begin to build upward. Use as many toothpicks and gumdrops as you like. This experiment is all about trial and error. Remember, this is a test of strength, not a race. Take it slow and think about it. There are precious gumdrops at stake!

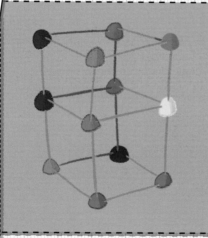

STEP 3

When your tower is as tall as you like, wait until everyone has finished. Nominate someone to be timekeeper and give them the stopwatch. Gently place your heavy book on top of each of the towers, one by one, and see how long they take to fall!

HOW DOES IT WORK?

Different parts of the gumdrop towers are pulling or pushing on each other all the time. The parts being pulled are in tension and the parts being squashed are in compression. When full-size buildings are designed, the engineers choose the materials according to the forces that will be acting on them. Look at what the buildings around where you live are made of. Certain materials, like bricks, don't squash easily so they are good at coping with compression forces. Other materials, like steel cables, don't break when they are stretched and can withstand tension forces. Your wooden toothpicks are strong under both compression and tension.

When you put the book on top of your gumdrop tower, you are applying a load to the structure, so when you design it there are several things to think about:

- Some shapes are stronger than others so think carefully about which to use.
- Some parts of your structure may have more force applied than others.
  See if you can decide which they are and how you could strengthen them.
- Sticking lots of toothpicks into a gumdrop joint may weaken it.
- The taller your structure is, the more important making it stable becomes.
  Structures with a wider base are more stable.

Ask yourself these questions:

- Which shapes are the strongest—squares, rectangles, or triangles?
- How could you change the base to give the tower more support?
- How can you make the joints strong and capable of withstanding weight?

CATAPULT BASKETBALL

Build your own basketball court and then challenge your friends to a game. It'll be a slam dunk!

YOU WILL NEED
- 1 large cardboard box
- 3 paper cups
- white glue
- 1 table tennis ball
- 1 milk bottle lid
- 7 craft sticks
- 4 rubber bands
- orange paint
- paintbrush
- markers
- scissors

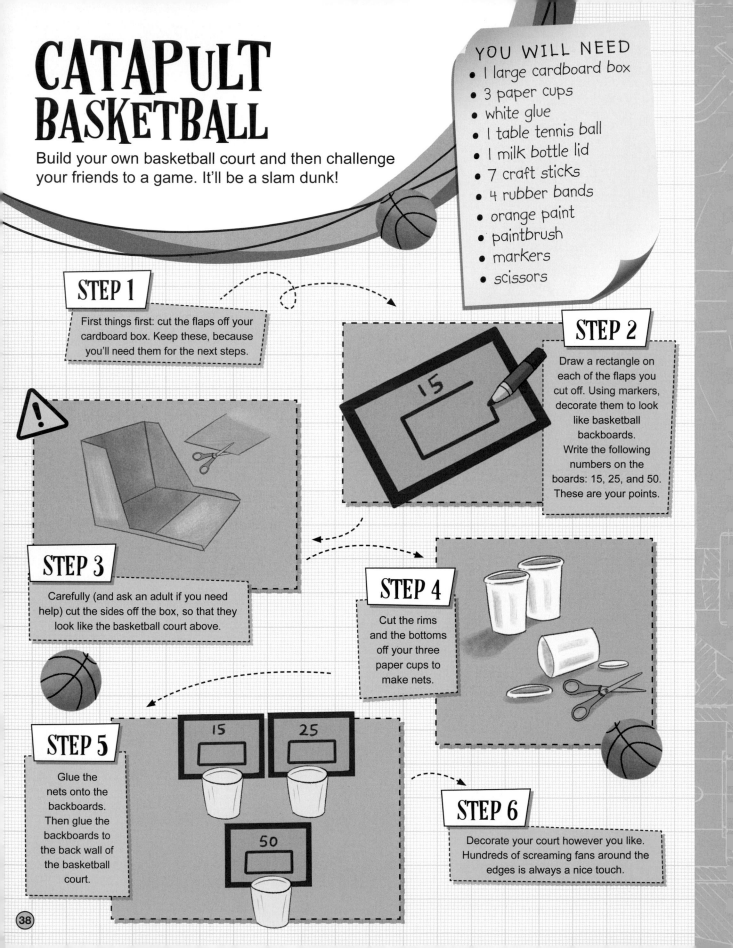

STEP 1
First things first: cut the flaps off your cardboard box. Keep these, because you'll need them for the next steps.

STEP 2
Draw a rectangle on each of the flaps you cut off. Using markers, decorate them to look like basketball backboards.
Write the following numbers on the boards: 15, 25, and 50. These are your points.

STEP 3
Carefully (and ask an adult if you need help) cut the sides off the box, so that they look like the basketball court above.

STEP 4
Cut the rims and the bottoms off your three paper cups to make nets.

STEP 5
Glue the nets onto the backboards. Then glue the backboards to the back wall of the basketball court.

STEP 6
Decorate your court however you like. Hundreds of screaming fans around the edges is always a nice touch.

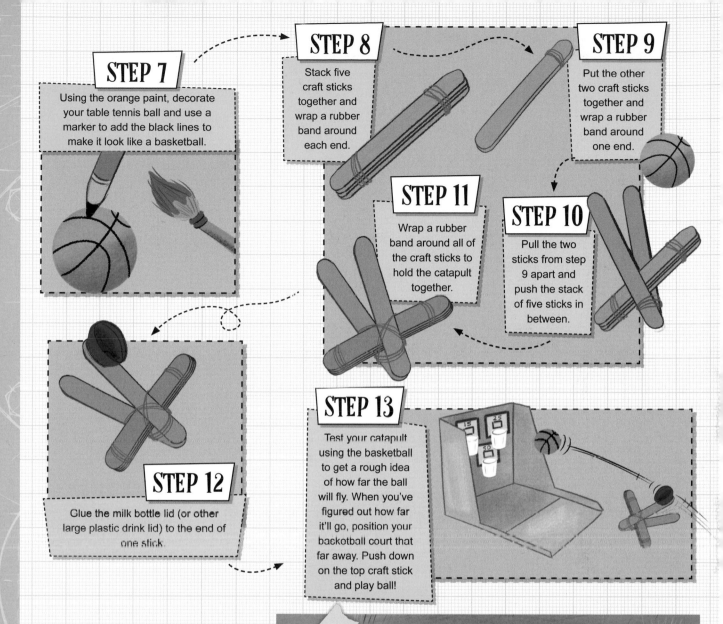

STEP 7

Using the orange paint, decorate your table tennis ball and use a marker to add the black lines to make it look like a basketball.

STEP 8

Stack five craft sticks together and wrap a rubber band around each end.

STEP 9

Put the other two craft sticks together and wrap a rubber band around one end.

STEP 11

Wrap a rubber band around all of the craft sticks to hold the catapult together.

STEP 10

Pull the two sticks from step 9 apart and push the stack of five sticks in between.

STEP 12

Glue the milk bottle lid (or other large plastic drink lid) to the end of one stick.

STEP 13

Test your catapult using the basketball to get a rough idea of how far the ball will fly. When you've figured out how far it'll go, position your basketball court that far away. Push down on the top craft stick and play ball!

HOW DOES IT WORK?

When you push down on the arm of the catapult, energy is stored in the rubber bands, and when you let go it is released and transferred into the ball, launching it into the air. The more you push down, the more energy is stored in the rubber bands, and the farther your ball will fly. As an engineer, you have to find the right force to give you a slam dunk every time.

MESSY RACERS

Be sure to take this OUTSIDE! It gets messy.

YOU WILL NEED

- plastic bottle with lid (a square bottle is best)
- 1 plastic straw
- 2 wooden skewers
- scissors
- baking soda
- tablespoon
- an adult with a hammer and nail
- 1 ¼ cups of vinegar
- 4 plastic bottle lids
- 8 metal washers
- modeling clay
- duct tape
- tissue paper

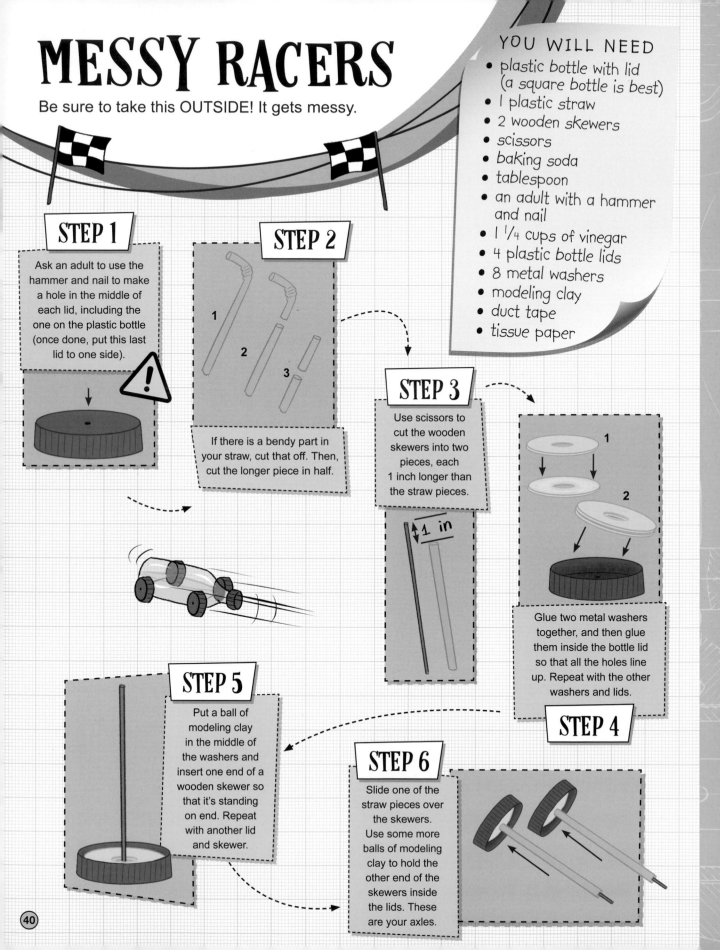

STEP 1

Ask an adult to use the hammer and nail to make a hole in the middle of each lid, including the one on the plastic bottle (once done, put this last lid to one side).

STEP 2

1

2

3

If there is a bendy part in your straw, cut that off. Then, cut the longer piece in half.

STEP 3

Use scissors to cut the wooden skewers into two pieces, each 1 inch longer than the straw pieces.

1 in

STEP 4

1

2

Glue two metal washers together, and then glue them inside the bottle lid so that all the holes line up. Repeat with the other washers and lids.

STEP 5

Put a ball of modeling clay in the middle of the washers and insert one end of a wooden skewer so that it's standing on end. Repeat with another lid and skewer.

STEP 6

Slide one of the straw pieces over the skewers. Use some more balls of modeling clay to hold the other end of the skewers inside the lids. These are your axles.

STEP 7

Use modeling clay to attach a wheel to the other end of each axle. Then use a piece of duct tape to stick the two axles to one side of the bottle. The lid-end of the bottle is the back of the car.

STEP 8

Go outside, twist open the bottle, and pour 1 ¼ cups of vinegar into the bottle.

STEP 9

Cut a 5-inch by 4-inch rectangle of tissue paper and pour in one tablespoon of baking soda. Roll up and fold the ends in so that the baking soda doesn't fall out.

STEP 10

Place bottle upright, insert the baking soda package into the bottle and QUICKLY close the lid. Shake the bottle. Place car wheels on the ground and let go!

WHAT NEXT?

You could conduct an experiment to find the best ratio of vinegar to baking soda. Measure the distance, time and direction it travels each time.

HOW DOES IT WORK?

Vinegar is an acid. Baking soda (also called sodium bicarbonate) is a type of chemical called a base. When they mix there is a vigorous reaction (you can see lots of bubbles and fizzing) and one of the chemicals formed is another acid called carbonic acid, which is used in soft drinks. The carbonic acid releases a gas called carbon dioxide (CO_2).

The pressure inside the bottle builds up from the CO_2 and pushes on the inside of the bottle in all directions. These forces would all cancel out but the hole in the bottle lid allows the gas to escape out the back of the car. There is nothing to cancel out the force on the inside of the front of the bottle, so the car moves forward.

BIG BUILDS

BIG BUILDS

If you want to throw yourself into a project and make something bold, beautiful, and BIG, then these experiments are perfect for you. They require all the skills of an engineer: planning, patience, precision, and minions to hold things and feed you snacks.

ROLLER COASTER RUN

Give a table tennis ball the ride of its boring little life by sending it speeding around a roller coaster track of your own design.

YOU WILL NEED
- pencil
- paper
- ruler
- 1 large cardboard box
- lots of straws
- scissors
- white glue
- 1 table tennis ball
- 1 paper bowl
- clear tape

PLANNING

STEP 1

Before you begin building, grab your pencil and paper, and sketch out some ideas for how you want your roller coaster to look. All good engineers plan first!

BUILDING THE TRACK

STEP 2

Tape your cardboard box closed and seal all the edges with clear tape.

STEP 3

Now you're ready to build. You should start from the end and work backward as this will make it easier. Put your paper bowl where you want your roller coaster to end and glue it in place.

STEP 4

Using the pointy end of your pencil, carefully make two holes in the box, 1 inch apart and 4 inches away from the paper bowl.

1 in   4 in

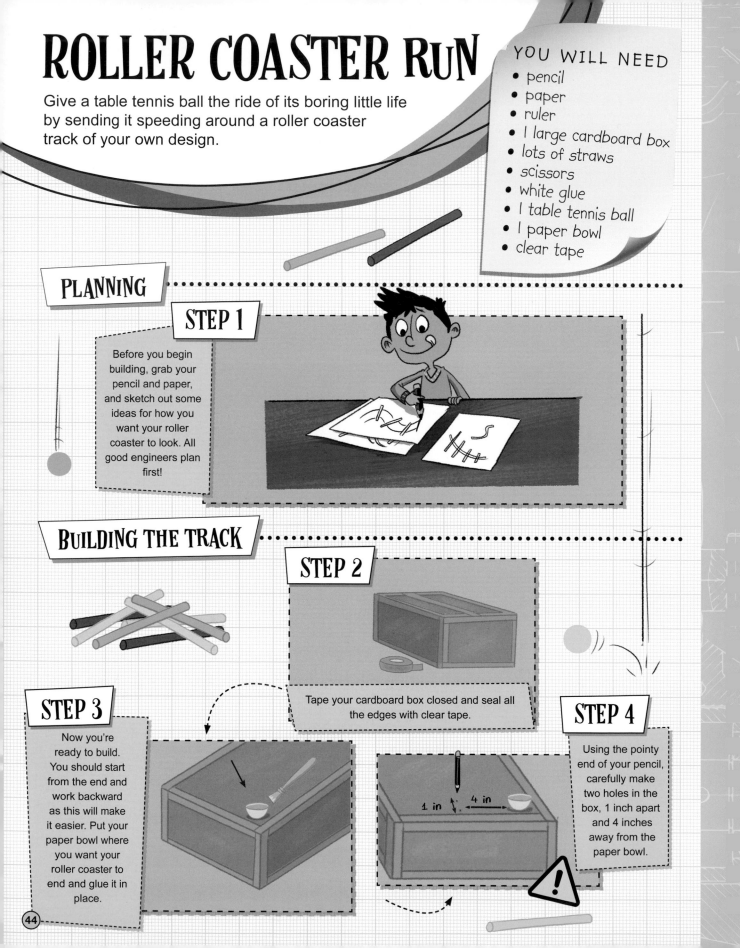

STEP 5

Carefully push a straw into each hole. Secure them in place by wrapping some clear tape around the bottoms, sticking them to the box. Using scissors, cut the straws so that they are 2 inches taller than your bowl. Don't throw away the cut off pieces of straw!

STEP 6

Cut a scrap piece of straw to make a 1-inch piece. Tape this in place just below the top of your two vertical straws, so that it joins them together. You have built your first track support!

STEP 7

To build the track, use two straws. Making sure one end of each straw overlaps the edge of your bowl, tape the other ends onto the horizontal support you added in step 6. This is your first track piece. Well done!

STEP 8

Engineering is trial and error, so you have to test your track. Put your ball at the top of track and let it go. It should roll straight into your bowl.

NEXT STEPS

As you build, you'll need to keep getting higher and higher, so that gravity pulls the ball downward. You can tape your straws together to build taller track supports, but the taller your rollercoaster gets, the more wobbly it'll become. Keep using your plan to guide you and test each piece as you go so that you can spot any problems before you've finished it all.

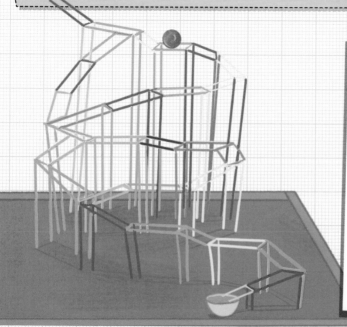

HOW DOES IT WORK?

When you lift the ball up at the start of the run, you're transferring energy into it. When you let it go and start it off on its downhill run, this energy gets transferred into movement. The higher it starts, the more energy it has.

Full-size roller coasters work like this, too. The train gets winched up by an electric motor and it then runs down, back to the start. The steeper the track, the faster the train—or the ball—will go. A great ride has some speed but it also lasts for several minutes. Can you keep your ball traveling for longer?

WAVE HELLO

Give yourself a massive thumbs up and wave boredom goodbye with this giant robotic hand.

YOU WILL NEED

- 5 paper towel tubes
- 1 large cereal box
- 5 pieces of string (23 inches each)
- clear tape
- 1 old glove
- 7 paper fasteners
- 1 pushpin
- white glue
- pencil
- scissors
- an adult

STEP 1

With a pencil, draw evenly placed diamond-shaped "joints" on all five tubes, leaving a little extra space at the bottom. There should be four finger tubes with three joints and one thumb tube with two.

STEP 2

Cut out the diamond shapes on all five tubes.

STEP 3

Cut 1/2 inch slits evenly around the bottom of all five tubes. Fold the tabs outwards.

STEP 4

Hold the thumb tube against the side of the cereal box at an angle (like your actual thumb). Use a pencil to mark the angle on the tube and then cut along that line.

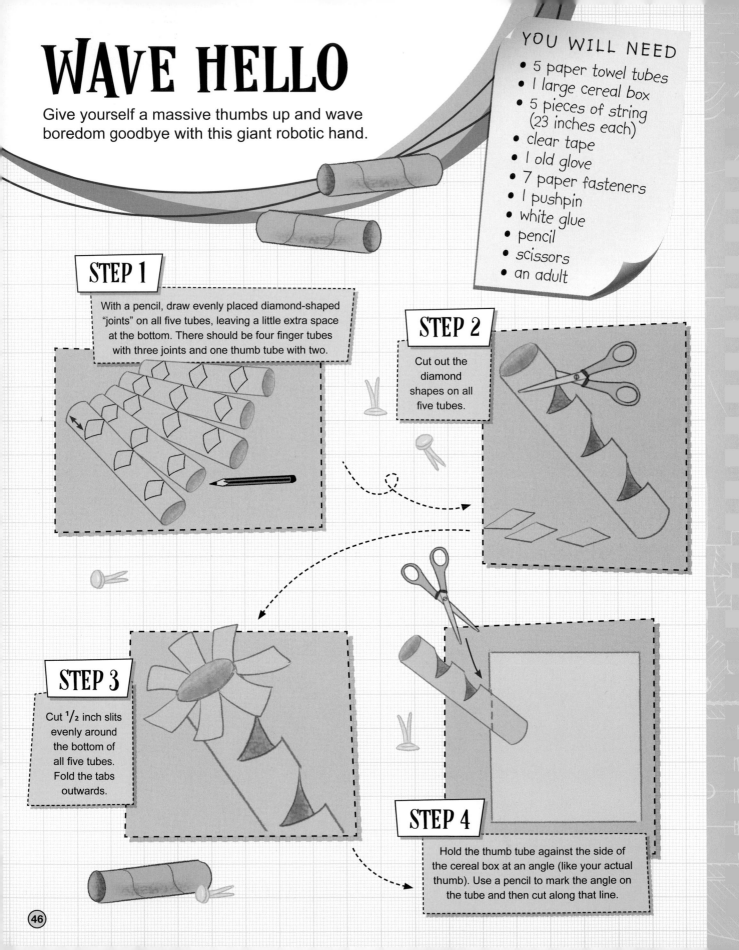

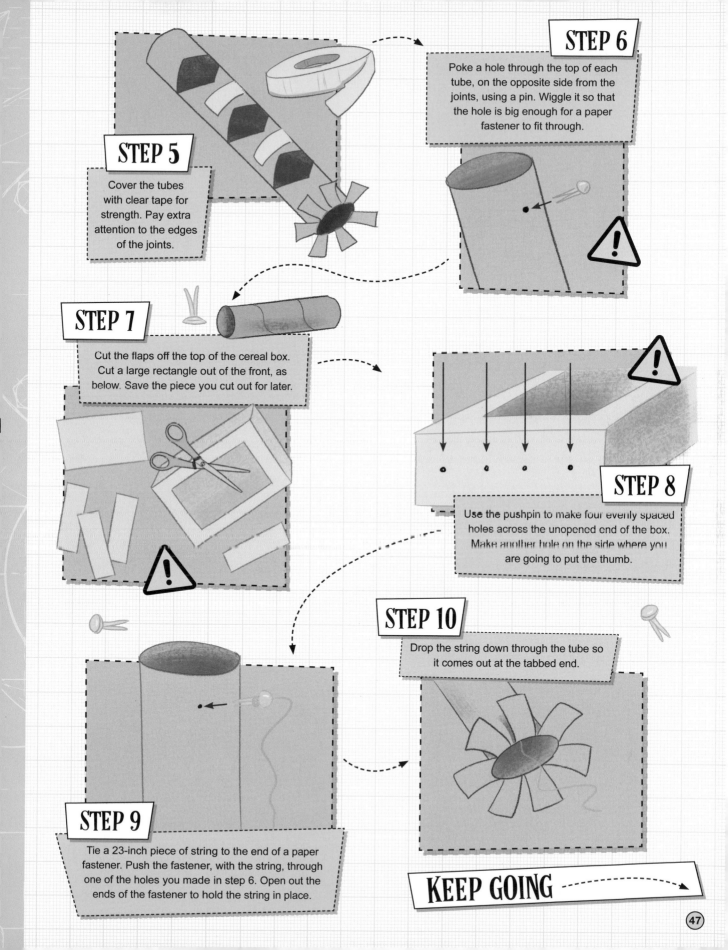

STEP 5

Cover the tubes with clear tape for strength. Pay extra attention to the edges of the joints.

STEP 6

Poke a hole through the top of each tube, on the opposite side from the joints, using a pin. Wiggle it so that the hole is big enough for a paper fastener to fit through.

STEP 7

Cut the flaps off the top of the cereal box. Cut a large rectangle out of the front, as below. Save the piece you cut out for later.

STEP 8

Use the pushpin to make four evenly spaced holes across the unopened end of the box. Make another hole on the side where you are going to put the thumb.

STEP 9

Tie a 23-inch piece of string to the end of a paper fastener. Push the fastener, with the string, through one of the holes you made in step 6. Open out the ends of the fastener to hold the string in place.

STEP 10

Drop the string down through the tube so it comes out at the tabbed end.

KEEP GOING

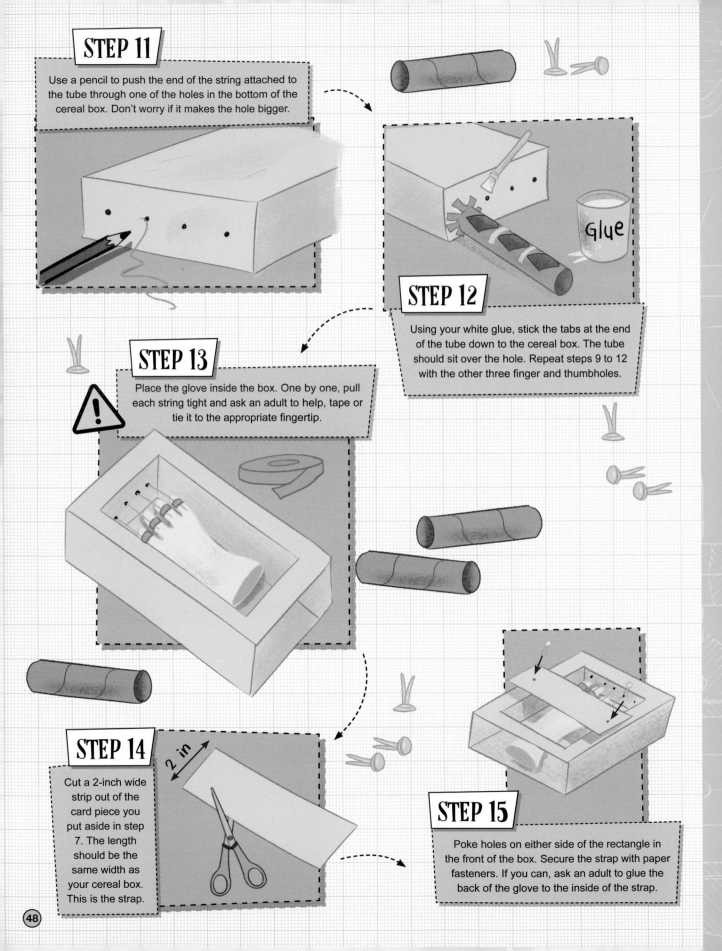

STEP 11

Use a pencil to push the end of the string attached to the tube through one of the holes in the bottom of the cereal box. Don't worry if it makes the hole bigger.

STEP 12

Using your white glue, stick the tabs at the end of the tube down to the cereal box. The tube should sit over the hole. Repeat steps 9 to 12 with the other three finger and thumbholes.

Glue

STEP 13

Place the glove inside the box. One by one, pull each string tight and ask an adult to help, tape or tie it to the appropriate fingertip.

STEP 14

Cut a 2-inch wide strip out of the card piece you put aside in step 7. The length should be the same width as your cereal box. This is the strap.

2 in

STEP 15

Poke holes on either side of the rectangle in the front of the box. Secure the strap with paper fasteners. If you can, ask an adult to glue the back of the glove to the inside of the strap.

Now put your hand in the glove and try curling your fingers. You can adjust the string tension by tightening or loosening the strings on the paper fasteners. The fingers may be a little stiff at first, but as you use them, the joints will crease and bend more easily. If the fingers still don't bend properly at the joints, try making the diamond-shaped cuts a little deeper.

HOW DOES IT WORK?

Sometimes engineers will base their designs around things found in nature, like your hand. This is called biomimetics. The strings in this robotic hand, for example, mimic the tendons found in your actual hand. Your muscles are joined to your bones by stringy fibers called tendons. When your muscles contract (squeeze), they pull on the tendons, which pull on the bones, bending your fingers. Your robotic hand works the same, with the string as tendons and the cardboard tubes as bones.

TURN THE MUSIC UP!

What was that? You want to make a really cool speaker out of cardboard to show off to your friends the next time they come over for a party? Alright, there's no need to shout …

STEP 1

Use a pencil and ruler to draw all the pieces you will need for this experiment on pieces of cardboard. Cut them out and set them to one side.

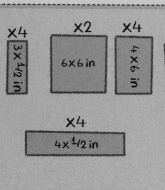

x4
3 x 1/2 in

x2
6 x 6 in

x4
4 x 6 in

x8
4 in
10 in
3/4 in

x4
4 x 1/2 in

STEP 2

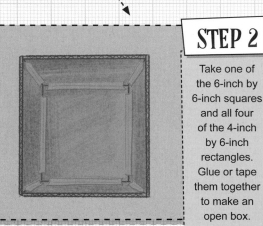

Take one of the 6-inch by 6-inch squares and all four of the 4-inch by 6-inch rectangles. Glue or tape them together to make an open box.

STEP 3

This is where you're going to need some patience, and probably your minion to help hold things. Grab all eight of your funnel-shaped pieces and start attaching the edges of each together one by one. You might want to use tape, since it will hold better and quicker, but glue will also work (you'll have to make your minion hold it for hours while it dries). As you stick the larger end of the funnel together, bend them into a slight curve. When you've finished, the eight pieces should connect together like an oddly shaped trumpet.

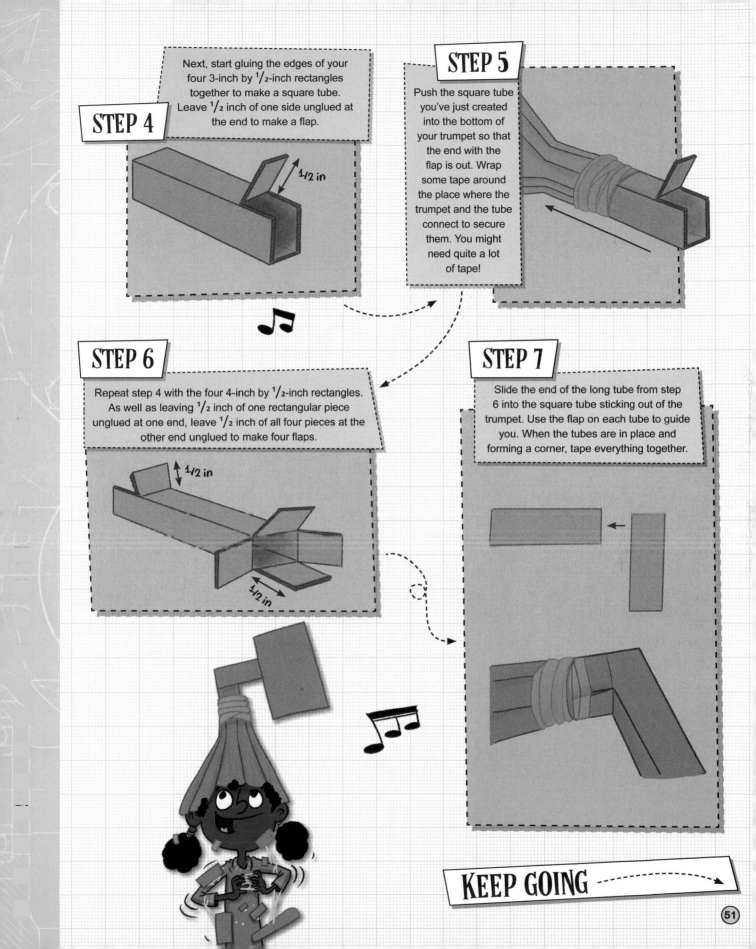

STEP 4

Next, start gluing the edges of your four 3-inch by $1/2$-inch rectangles together to make a square tube. Leave $1/2$ inch of one side unglued at the end to make a flap.

$1/2$ in

STEP 5

Push the square tube you've just created into the bottom of your trumpet so that the end with the flap is out. Wrap some tape around the place where the trumpet and the tube connect to secure them. You might need quite a lot of tape!

STEP 6

Repeat step 4 with the four 4-inch by $1/2$-inch rectangles. As well as leaving $1/2$ inch of one rectangular piece unglued at one end, leave $1/2$ inch of all four pieces at the other end unglued to make four flaps.

$1/2$ in

$1/2$ in

STEP 7

Slide the end of the long tube from step 6 into the square tube sticking out of the trumpet. Use the flap on each tube to guide you. When the tubes are in place and forming a corner, tape everything together.

KEEP GOING

STEP 8

To make the lid of the box, measure the width and depth of your smartphone. On the other 6-inch by 6-inch square, cut two holes: one should be a ¹/₂-inch by ¹/₂-inch square and the one below that should be just slightly bigger than the width and depth of your smartphone. You might need to ask an adult to help with this.

¹/2 in

¹/2 in

STEP 9

Push the end of the tube from step 7 through the ¹/₂-inch by ¹/₂-inch hole. Bend the flaps outward and tape them all down to the underside of the lid.

STEP 10

Carefully glue the lid to the open box you made in step 2. You might need some minion-help with this, to hold the lid and trumpet while you glue it onto the box.

STEP 11

Get some music playing on a smartphone and slide the phone into the slot in the lid. Put on your dancing shoes and boogie!

HOW DOES IT WORK?

Sound waves get quieter as they spread out. So they sound louder if you can funnel them together. The sounds from your smartphone's speaker bounce along the tube and out into the funnel, which directs them in a tight beam toward the dance floor. This makes the music sound louder if you're in line with the funnel, but makes it harder to hear elsewhere.

YOU WILL NEED

- white glue
- 1 wooden skewer
- 10 craft sticks
- cardboard sheets
- 2 plastic syringes
- 2 zip ties
- colored LED battery light
- 12 inch plastic tubing
- an adult with a drill
- bowl of water
- markers
- paper
- scissors
- ruler

TRICK, TREAT, OR TERROR?

Halloween is the perfect time to give your friends a little scare. But the beauty of this experiment is that it can scare all year round.

STEP 1

Using scissors, cut the rounded ends off one craft stick and then cut it into seven roughly equal pieces. Glue the pieces one on top of the other. Repeat with nine more craft sticks, so you have ten stacks.

STEP 2

Cut out four squares from the cardboard sheets. The squares should be 8 inches by 8 inches

8 in   8 in

STEP 3

Glue the four squares together to make the bottom and three sides of a box.

Glue

STEP 4

Ask an adult to drill holes through the middle of eight of your stacks. Leave two undrilled.

STEP 5

Glue two of the stacks with holes to the inside edges of the box, as shown. The holes in the stacks should be facing inward.

hole

STEP 6

Cut your wooden skewer so that it's 7 ½ inches long.

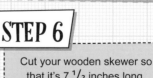

KEEP GOING - - - - - ▶

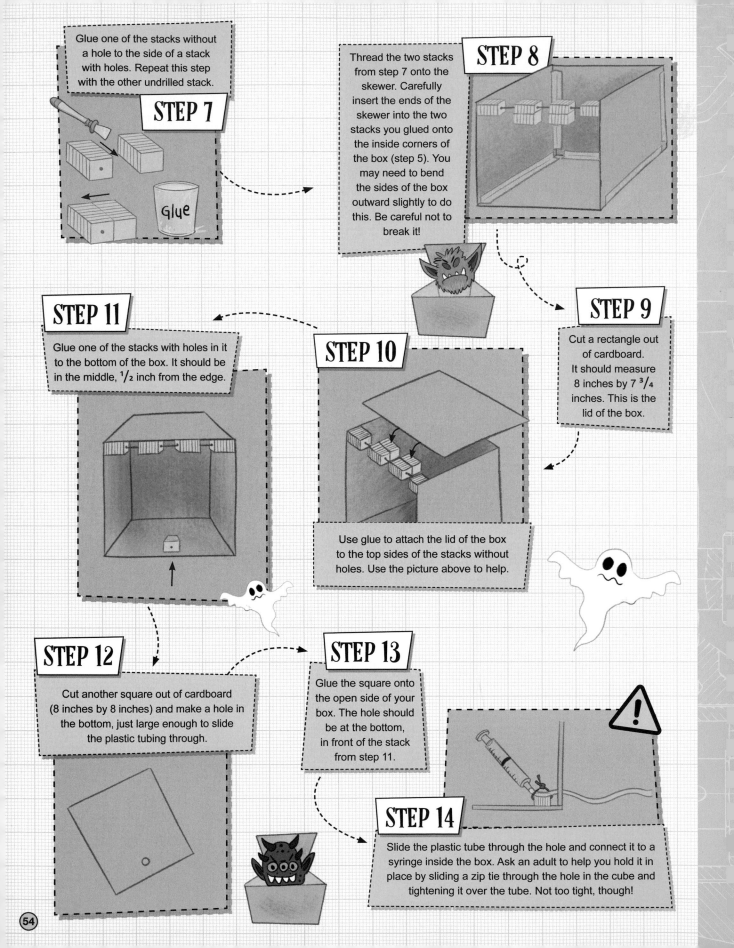

STEP 7

Glue one of the stacks without a hole to the side of a stack with holes. Repeat this step with the other undrilled stack.

Glue

STEP 8

Thread the two stacks from step 7 onto the skewer. Carefully insert the ends of the skewer into the two stacks you glued onto the inside corners of the box (step 5). You may need to bend the sides of the box outward slightly to do this. Be careful not to break it!

STEP 9

Cut a rectangle out of cardboard. It should measure 8 inches by 7 $\frac{3}{4}$ inches. This is the lid of the box.

STEP 10

Use glue to attach the lid of the box to the top sides of the stacks without holes. Use the picture above to help.

STEP 11

Glue one of the stacks with holes in it to the bottom of the box. It should be in the middle, $\frac{1}{2}$ inch from the edge.

STEP 12

Cut another square out of cardboard (8 inches by 8 inches) and make a hole in the bottom, just large enough to slide the plastic tubing through.

STEP 13

Glue the square onto the open side of your box. The hole should be at the bottom, in front of the stack from step 11.

STEP 14

Slide the plastic tube through the hole and connect it to a syringe inside the box. Ask an adult to help you hold it in place by sliding a zip tie through the hole in the cube and tightening it over the tube. Not too tight, though!

STEP 15

Glue a stack with a hole in to the end of the syringe inside the box.

STEP 16

Glue the last stack to the underside of your lid, in the middle, $1/2$ inch from the edge. Ask your trained adult to help you zip tie the stack inside the lid to the one on the end of the syringe.

STEP 17

Fill the other syringe with water and attach it to the other end of the tubing.

STEP 18

Put your LED light into the box. On a piece of paper, use your markers to draw the spookiest ghost possible, cut it out, and glue the back of the ghost's head to the front of the stack on the lid. When the lid closes, the ghost should sit neatly inside the box.

STEP 19

Push down the plunger on the syringe and watch in amazement as the water moves through the tube and into the other syringe in the box, pushing the plunger out and raising the lid!

HOW DOES IT WORK?

A hinge is a movable joint that lets something open and close. The lid of your box can move up and down because of the hinge joint. There are examples of hinges around your house: doors, windows, and gates are connected by hinges.

As you push on the syringe, the water inside has nowhere to go and the pressure builds up. This pressure causes the plunger in the other syringe to move outwards. Because the lid is built on a hinge, when the plunger moves outward, it also pushes the lid up. Hydraulic systems, which use water to create movement, are very powerful, and are used in machines like diggers and dumper trucks.

SAFE AND SOUND

Use this combination safe to keep all your secrets and valuables away from prying eyes. After all, there are some nosy people around (looking at you, little sibling).

If you have a hot glue gun and an adult to wield it, this project might be easier.

STEP 1

Cut a 5-inch by 5-inch square out of cardboard. Using a pencil and ruler, draw a square in the center of the 5-inch square. It should be 1 inch from each edge. Carefully cut out the square in the middle.

5 in · 1 in · 5 in · 5 in

STEP 2

Carefully, on one edge of the inner square, cut a 1/2-inch square notch into the edge. It doesn't matter where you cut it.

STEP 3

Cut another square of cardboard that's 3 1/2 inches by 3 1/2 inches.

STEP 5

Glue the 2 1/2-inch square of cardboard to the center of the 3 1/2-inch square you made in step 3 using white glue.

LOOT

Glu

STEP 4

2 1/2 in · 2 1/2 in

You've guessed it, cut yet another square. This time, it should be 2 1/2 inches by 2 1/2 inches.

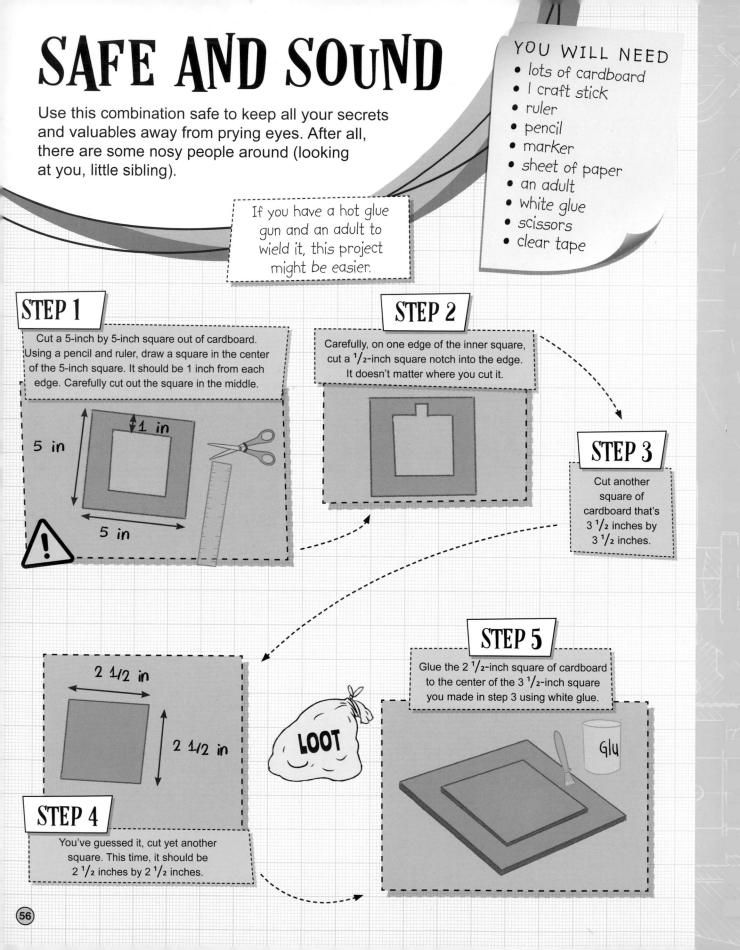

STEP 6

Cut a 11 ³/₄-inch by 2-inch strip of paper and roll it tightly around a pencil into a tube. Glue the end so that it doesn't unravel.

Cut the tube so that it is ³/₄ inch long.

STEP 7

3/4 in

STEP 8

Ask your adult to make a hole in the center of the glued cardboard squares from step 4. It needs to be wide enough to comfortably fit your paper tube.

TREASURE

STEP 9

Push the little tube through the hole.

STEP 10

Cut out a 2-inch-wide circle out of cardboard to make a dial. Using a marker, add numbers to your dial. Go up in increments of five and add in little lines for the numbers in between.

0 5 10 15 20 25 30 35

Glue

KEEP GOING

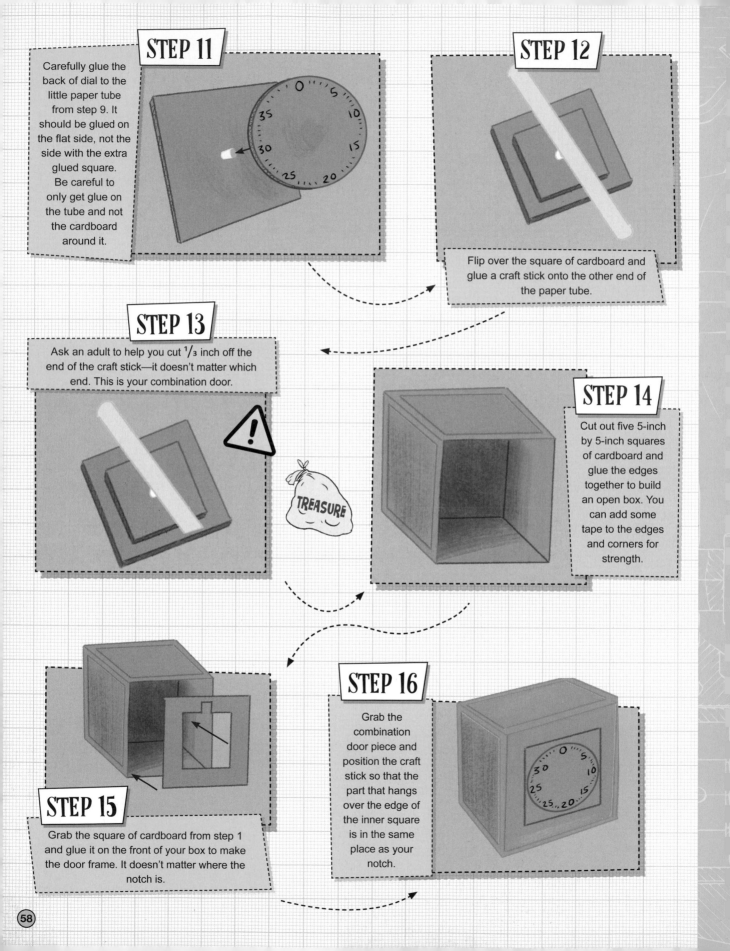

STEP 11

Carefully glue the back of dial to the little paper tube from step 9. It should be glued on the flat side, not the side with the extra glued square. Be careful to only get glue on the tube and not the cardboard around it.

STEP 12

Flip over the square of cardboard and glue a craft stick onto the other end of the paper tube.

STEP 13

Ask an adult to help you cut $\frac{1}{3}$ inch off the end of the craft stick—it doesn't matter which end. This is your combination door.

TREASURE

STEP 14

Cut out five 5-inch by 5-inch squares of cardboard and glue the edges together to build an open box. You can add some tape to the edges and corners for strength.

STEP 15

Grab the square of cardboard from step 1 and glue it on the front of your box to make the door frame. It doesn't matter where the notch is.

STEP 16

Grab the combination door piece and position the craft stick so that the part that hangs over the edge of the inner square is in the same place as your notch.

STEP 17

Using strips of cardboard, glue a couple of hinges to your door to keep it in place.

LOOT

STEP 18

Use your marker to draw a small arrow on the door above the dial in the middle. You will need to line up your secret combination with this arrow to open the safe.

STEP 19

To figure out your secret combination, slowly turn the dial, increment by increment, until the overhanging end of the craft stick lines up inside with the notch in the frame and the door opens! Remember the number or write it down on a piece of paper and hide it somewhere. Now fill your safe with all your treasures!

HOW DOES IT WORK?

The door won't open unless the craft stick is lined up with the notch in the frame. The position of the craft stick is controlled by the dial. The dial has to be turned to the correct position for the stick to pass through the gap. The position of the dial can be set by the numbers—but only you know the right number to line up with the arrow.

BUILD A CRANE

Create a construction site in your own house with some BIG fun, all in the name of science!

YOU WILL NEED
- cardboard
- wooden skewers
- string
- 1 clean yogurt container
- modeling clay
- scissors
- pencil
- ruler
- white glue
- an adult

STEP 1

This is going to be a big first step, so it's time to bring out those impressive cardboard-cutting skills. Use a pencil and ruler to draw all the pieces you will need and then cut them out and lay them to one side.

8 1/2 in
×4
1 1/2 in
×6
3/4 in
4 in
×2
×2
3/4 in
1 1/2 in
×4
3 1/4 in
2 1/4 in
4 in
4 in
×2
4 in
×2
3 1/2 in
1 in
1 in
×2
1 1/2 in
1 1/2 in

STEP 2

Glue two of the long 8 1/4-inch by 1 1/2-inch pieces with arches on the end together. Repeat with the other two. These will be the arms of the crane.

STEP 3

Glue two of the 3 1/4-inch by 2 1/4-inch arches back to back. Repeat this step with the other two arches of the same size.

STEP 5

Glue the other 4-inch by 4-inch square onto the top of your open box.

STEP 4

Using one of the 4-inch by 4-inch squares as the base, glue the bottom of the 4-inch by 1-inch and the 3 1/2-inch by 1-inch rectangles onto the sides to make a shallow box.

4 in
3 1/2 in
3 1/2 in
4 in

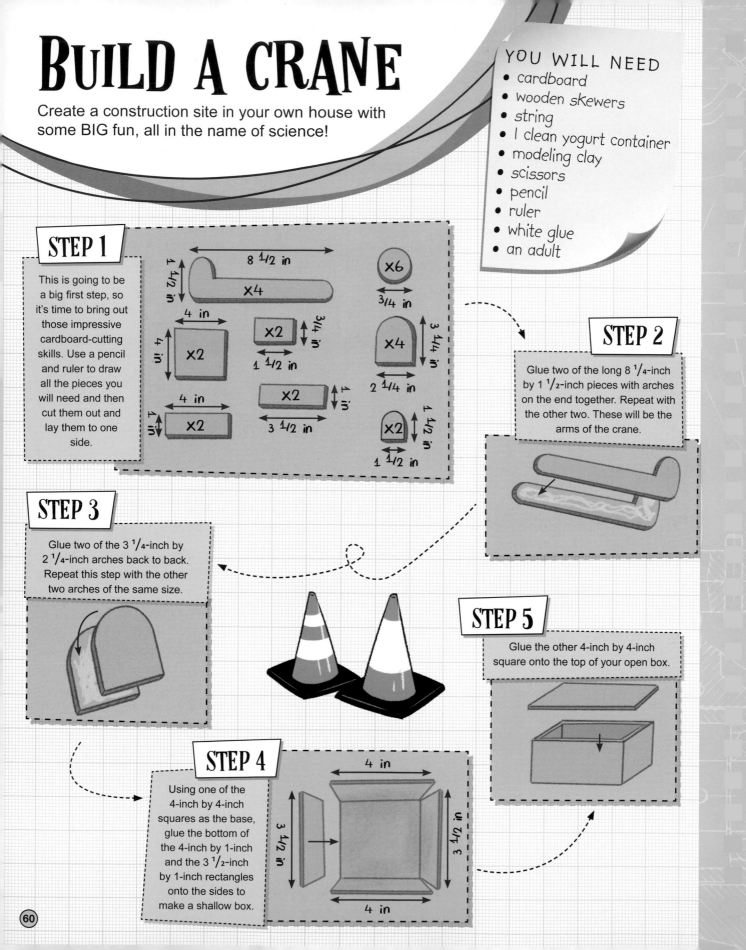

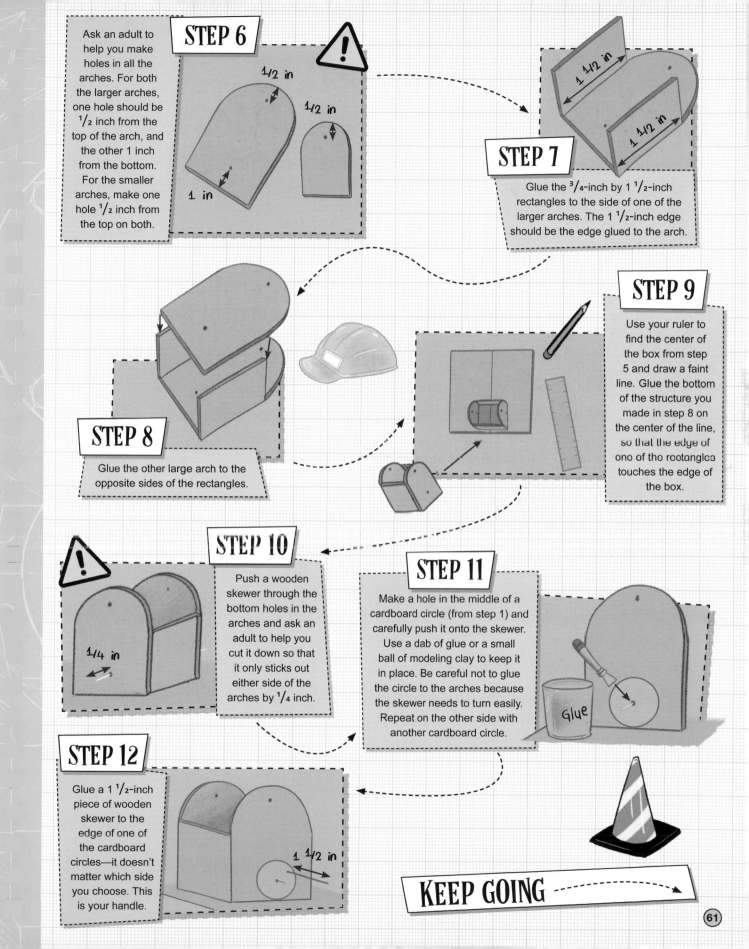

STEP 6

Ask an adult to help you make holes in all the arches. For both the larger arches, one hole should be $\frac{1}{2}$ inch from the top of the arch, and the other 1 inch from the bottom. For the smaller arches, make one hole $\frac{1}{2}$ inch from the top on both.

$\frac{1}{2}$ in

$\frac{1}{2}$ in

1 in

STEP 7

Glue the $\frac{3}{4}$-inch by 1 $\frac{1}{2}$-inch rectangles to the side of one of the larger arches. The 1 $\frac{1}{2}$-inch edge should be the edge glued to the arch.

1 $\frac{1}{2}$ in

1 $\frac{1}{2}$ in

STEP 9

Use your ruler to find the center of the box from step 5 and draw a faint line. Glue the bottom of the structure you made in step 8 on the center of the line, so that the edge of one of the rectangles touches the edge of the box.

STEP 8

Glue the other large arch to the opposite sides of the rectangles.

STEP 10

Push a wooden skewer through the bottom holes in the arches and ask an adult to help you cut it down so that it only sticks out either side of the arches by $\frac{1}{4}$ inch.

$\frac{1}{4}$ in

STEP 11

Make a hole in the middle of a cardboard circle (from step 1) and carefully push it onto the skewer. Use a dab of glue or a small ball of modeling clay to keep it in place. Be careful not to glue the circle to the arches because the skewer needs to turn easily. Repeat on the other side with another cardboard circle.

Glue

STEP 12

Glue a 1 $\frac{1}{2}$-inch piece of wooden skewer to the edge of one of the cardboard circles—it doesn't matter which side you choose. This is your handle.

1 $\frac{1}{2}$ in

KEEP GOING

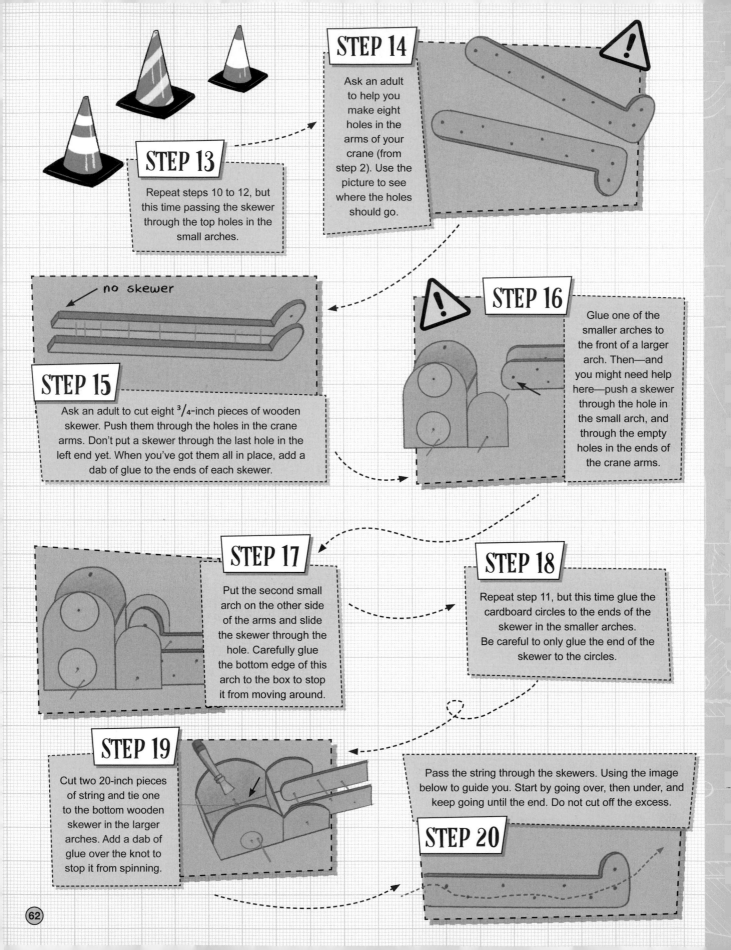

STEP 13

Repeat steps 10 to 12, but this time passing the skewer through the top holes in the small arches.

STEP 14

Ask an adult to help you make eight holes in the arms of your crane (from step 2). Use the picture to see where the holes should go.

no skewer

STEP 15

Ask an adult to cut eight ³/₄-inch pieces of wooden skewer. Push them through the holes in the crane arms. Don't put a skewer through the last hole in the left end yet. When you've got them all in place, add a dab of glue to the ends of each skewer.

STEP 16

Glue one of the smaller arches to the front of a larger arch. Then—and you might need help here—push a skewer through the hole in the small arch, and through the empty holes in the ends of the crane arms.

STEP 17

Put the second small arch on the other side of the arms and slide the skewer through the hole. Carefully glue the bottom edge of this arch to the box to stop it from moving around.

STEP 18

Repeat step 11, but this time glue the cardboard circles to the ends of the skewer in the smaller arches. Be careful to only glue the end of the skewer to the circles.

STEP 19

Cut two 20-inch pieces of string and tie one to the bottom wooden skewer in the larger arches. Add a dab of glue over the knot to stop it from spinning.

STEP 20

Pass the string through the skewers. Using the image below to guide you. Start by going over, then under, and keep going until the end. Do not cut off the excess.

STEP 21

Tie another piece of string to the middle of the top skewer in the large arches and glue. Pull the string taut and glue it to the top horizontal skewer in between the large arches. Make sure the string is not slack and cut off any excess.

STEP 22

Cut four 5-inch pieces of string. Glue the pieces of string to the sides of your empty yogurt container to make a handle. Tie the long, dangling piece of string from step 20 to the handle.

STEP 23

The top reel controls the arm of the crane, making it move up and down. The bottom reel controls the up and down of the bucket (your yogurt container). So, fill it up with your most precious and unbreakable cargo, and get lifting!

HOW DOES IT WORK?

A crane is all about forces. The string attached to the top reel raises and lowers the arm of the crane (sometimes called the jib). If you pull on the string it applies a force to raise it and if you release the string, then gravity will pull the arm down. The string attached to the bottom reel is attached to the load. This will raise and lower it in the same way. You supply the force to raise it and gravity will do the work on the way down.

DIFFERENT TYPES OF ENGINEERS

Different types of engineers specialize in different things. As you worked through this book, you performed the same job as all of these engineers at least once.

AUTOMOTIVE ENGINEERS

An automotive engineer designs the vehicles we use every day.

- Wheelie Fun! – page 10
- Messy Racers – page 40
- Build a Crane – page 60

BIOMEDICAL ENGINEERS

Biomedical engineers design and test medical equipment that works with the human body.

- Monster Jaws – page 8
- Wave Hello – page 46

MARINE ENGINEERS

A marine engineer designs, builds, tests, and repairs machines that go in water.

- Paddle Away – page 14

CHEMICAL ENGINEERS

Chemical engineers use science to change chemicals into more useful or valuable things.

- Super Boing! – page 18
- Messy Racers – page 40

STRUCTURAL ENGINEERS

Structural engineers design buildings to make sure they stay standing, even during natural disasters.

- Roll Up, Roll Up – page 28
- Gumdrop Towers – page 36
- Roller Coaster Run – page 44

AEROSPACE ENGINEERS

Aerospace engineers design, build, and test, machines that fly and go into space.

- Blast Off! – page 16
- Eggs Away! – page 20